THE CAHUILLA LANDSCAPE
The Santa Rosa and San Jacinto Mountains

Pedro Chino, Cahuilla Shaman, and His Dog in Chino Canyon
April, 1939

Ballena Press Anthropological Papers No. 37
Editor: Sylvia Brakke Vane

THE CAHUILLA LANDSCAPE

The Santa Rosa and San Jacinto Mountains

by

Lowell John Bean, Sylvia Brakke Vane, and Jackson Young

with

Contributions by

Bern Schwenn

BALLENA PRESS
823 Valparaiso Avenue
Menlo Park, California 94025

Ballena Press General Editors: Sylvia Brakke Vane and Lowell John Bean

Volume Editor: Karla Young

Ballena Press Anthropological Papers Editors:
>   **Thomas C. Blackburn**
>   **Sylvia Brakke Vane**
>   **Lowell John Bean**

Library of Congress Cataloging-in-Publication Data

Bean, Lowell John.
　　The Cahuilla Landscape : The Santa Rosa and
San Jacinto Mountains / Lowell John Bean, Sylvia
Brakke Vane, and Jackson Young, with contributions
by Bern Schwenn.
　　　　p. cm. -- (Ballena Press anthropological papers ;
　　no. 37) Includes bibliographical references and index.
　　ISBN 0-87919-121-X : $19.95. -- ISBN 0-87919-120-1
　　(pbk.) : $14.95
　　　1. Cahuilla Indians--Antiquities. 2. Cahuilla Indians--
Names. 3. Names, Geographical--California--Santa Rosa
Mountains. 4. Names, Geographical--California--San Jacinto
Mountains. 5. Land settlement patterns--California--Santa Rosa
Mountains. 6. Land settlement patterns--California--San
Jacinto Mountains. 7. Santa Rosa Mountains (Calif.)--
Antiquities. 8. San Jacinto Mountains (Calif.)--Antiquities.
9. California--Antiquities. I. Vane, Sylvia Brakke,
II. Young, Jackson. III. Title. IV. Series.
E99.C155B417 1991
979.4'9--dc20　　　　　　　　　　　　　91-8148
　　　　　　　　　　　　　　　　　　　CIP

Printed in the United States of America

First Printing

"All the places in the mountains and the flat land are named and known to the Indians. A hunter can return, leaving extra loads of game, and any man that he sends back always finds and brings it home."

Francisco Patencio 1943:99

TABLE OF CONTENTS

TABLE OF ILLUSTRATIONS

MAPS

I. FOREWORD

by

Russell L. Kaldenberg and Richard Milanovich

We appreciate the honor of being asked to write a foreword to this important document on the Santa Rosa and San Jacinto Mountains. The reader should be aware that the Santa Rosa Mountains (and the San Jacinto Mountains) are extremely significant to the Cahuilla people. They provided food, shelter, and spiritual places for generations of native peoples before the arrival of Euro-Americans in the Coachella Valley of California. The mountains still provide the Cahuilla people with many of the basic necessities of life.

The Santa Rosa Mountains are also important to Euro-America. Their topographic relief provide the striking background to the Coachella Valley, scenery that is unparalleled anywhere in California. By the very nature of settlement and land allocation after California attained statehood in 1850, the ownership pattern in the mountains became a co-mingling of private, public, and Indian lands. A portion of the western Santa Rosa Mountains were designated as the San Bernardino National Forest early in the 20th century. The Anza-Borrego and San Jacinto State Parks were also created in parts of the mountain range. The Agua Caliente and Morongo Reservations are within portions of the Santa Rosa Mountains. The Torres-Martinez Reservation is at the eastern base of the range. Within a portion of the Santa Rosa Mountains the Santa Rosa Indian Reservation also exists. Lands managed by the Bureau of Land Management and the State of California, and various private lands comprise the rest of the ownership.

The Santa Rosa Mountains were designated as a National Scenic Areas by the Secretary of the Interior in 1990. This historic action was the result of several persons and groups meeting together to talk about the significance of the Santa Rosa Mountains and the onslaught of population growth in the Coachella Valley. After several meetings it was evident that there was widespread support for a partnership to be developed to discuss and plan for the future of the mountains. Bureau of Land Management staff spent many days meeting with representatives of various cities, organizations, and special interest groups concerning the mountains. Through the discussions came a consensus that something special should be done to provide a management umbrella which would provide for the preservation and public use of the Santa Rosas in a uniform manner along with a formal recognition of the unique qualities of the mountains.

All nine cities, the County of Riverside, and the Agua Caliente and Morongo Reservations joined together to become partners in the formation of the Santa Rosa Mountains National Scenic Area, the fourth such scenic area in the United States. From its inception to its dedication on Cinco de Mayo 1990 the designation took less than one year. This is a tribute not only to the partnership, but to the importance of the mountain range.

A steering committee consisting of representatives of various cities, interest groups, Indian tribes, and the Bureau of Land Management was established in late 1990 with the goal of developing a long term plan which will guide the management of the mountains for decades to come. The principal resources to be protected are viewshed, native cultural sites. wildlife such as bighorn sheep and the slender-toed salamander, hiking experiences and just knowing that there is a buffer from the urban landscape which is engulfing southern California. The majority of the mountains are available only on foot and the plan is to keep them that way.

The partnerships created are long term. Management of the mountains require this to be so. In order for complete success to occur a diligent effort must be made to consolidate the lands into public ownership. This will be done through land exchanges, purchases, and strict adherence to open space standards by local governmental entities.

We, who have been active since the beginning of the creation of the National Scenic Area, encourage the reader to participate in the history of the living mountains, enjoying the rugged landscape and all the while respecting the sacredness of this special place. This book serves to tie in the scenic area to its land base.

Russell L. Kaldenberg
Area Manager, Palm Springs
Bureau of Land Management

Richard Milanovich
Tribal Chairman
Agua Caliente Band of Cahuilla Indians

PARTICIPANTS

Cities

Palm Springs
Desert Hot Springs
Cathedral City
Indian Wells
Rancho Mirage
Palm Desert
Indio
La Quinta
Coachella

County of Riverside
State of California, Department of Fish & Game
  Wildlife Conservation Board
  University of California, Deep Canyon Research
  Station
Bighorn Institute
Living Desert Reserve
Palm Springs Desert Museum
Palm Springs Open Space & Trials (POST)
Friends of the Indian Canyons
The Nature Conservancy
Snow Creek Property Owners Association
Pinyon Crest Property Owners Association

Department of the Interior

Agua Caliente Band of Cahuilla Indians
Morongo Band of Cahuilla Indians

Bureau of Land Management

II. ACKNOWLEDGEMENTS

We wish first of all to thank Russell Kaldenberg and Richard Milanovich for writing the Foreword to this book and associating it with the establishment of the Santa Rosa Mountains National Scenic Area. Indeed, we are indebted to them in more ways than that. It was Russell Kaldenberg who suggested that we undertake the revision and republication as a Ballena Press book of *The Cahuilla and the Santa Rosa Mountain Region: Places and Their Native American Associations, a Review of Published and Unpublished Resources* (Bean, Vane, and Young 1981), originally prepared for the U.S. Department of the Interior, Bureau of Land Management (BLM), Desert Planning Staff, Riverside, California. It is largely because we have had the opportunity to conduct a number of cultural resource management studies on lands owned by the Agua Caliente Band of Mission Indians, of which Richard Milanovich is Tribal Chairman, that we know a great deal more about the Santa Rosa and San Jacinto Mountains now than we did in 1981.

Like the previous volume, this book has been authored by Lowell John Bean, Ph.D., Sylvia Brakke Vane, M.A., and Jackson Young. Bern Schwenn, M.A., a geologist and an expert on the trails of the Santa Rosa and San Jacinto Mountains, has assisted in the research for this revised version. Because she is familiar with the mountain trails, she has been able to help us locate places named in the literature with much greater precision than we previously could, and has mapped them for us. In addition, she has had a major role in assembling information about places from additional literature sources.

As scholars we have organized the information and written it down. The information was provided by Native Americans--those who talked to us and those who talked to our predecessors. Those whom we consulted while doing the original study and more recently for this revised version include the late Mariano Saubel, the late Matthew Pablo, and the late Eugene Pablo of Morongo Indian Reservation; Richard Milanovich and Anthony Andreas, Jr. of the Agua Caliente Band of Cahuilla Indians; Anthony Largo of Santa Rosa Indian Reservation; the late Alice Torro Lopez, Saturnino Torro, and the late Ruby Modesto of the Torres-Martinez Indian Reservation; and Katherine Siva Saubel and Alvino Siva of Los Coyotes Indian Reservation. A number of other Native Americans, now deceased, with whom we consulted in years past, contributed to our understanding of Cahuilla culture, and our knowledge of Cahuilla places. These included Victoria Wierick, Jane Penn, Juan Siva, Calistro Tortes, Cinciona Lubo, and others. We appreciate knowing or having known them all. This book would not have been possible without the information--and the encouragement and support--they have given us.

Native Americans who provided the information in various published ethnographic works have also contributed a great deal to this book. First and foremost was Francisco Patencio, who provided the Cahuilla names for so many of the places we have listed (Patencio 1943; 1971). Second was his brother Alejo Patencio, who gave a great many place names and other information to Strong (1929). August Lomas, Francisco Nombre, Jolian Lopez, Akasem Levi, Rosa Morongo, Jesusa Manuel, Alec Arguello, and Alexander Arguello provided Strong (1929) with other data. Gifford (1918) talked to Captain Jim and his son Will Jim of Coachella, Maria Augustine, Francisco Torres and Chapo Levi.

We wish to express our appreciation also to the Palm Springs Historical Society, the Palm Springs Desert Museum, the Agua Caliente Band of Cahuilla Indians, Russell Kaldenberg, and

Anthony J. Andreas, Jr., all of whom let us examine their collections of photographs and use those that fit our purposes.

Appreciation is also due Drew Pallette and other members of the Coachella Valley Archaeological Association for helping make the color photography possible, and for continuing support and encouragement.

We shall not list here all the other scholars from whose work we've drawn information, as the "References Cited" will provide those names. We owe a tremendous debt to them for having preserved so much information that would otherwise have gone to the grave with the elders who knew it.

The archivists and librarians who have helped us acquire data from unpublished material and rare published works through the years will also remain unnamed, but their contributions are nonetheless greatly appreciated.

Others who contributed to this book were the members of our support staff, especially Ernest Quinones, Theresa Cicchinelli, Karla Young, and Arthur B. Vane, who have been responsible for scanning the original work onto computer files, and a great deal of editing, typing, indexing, and proof reading.

III. INTRODUCTION

What a challenge it is to put together a book on the place names with which the Cahuilla organized their landscape! If our goal were to record every place name known, we should find it an impossible challenge, for the Cahuilla had names for hundreds of features within each lineage's territory. Fortunately for our chances of meeting the challenge, our goal is to record only the most prominent places--the village and settlement sites, the most important mountains, springs, and lakes, and the places recalled in migration stories and other oral literature.

This book had its beginning in a cultural resource management report published by the Bureau of Land Management, *The Cahuilla and the Santa Rosa Mountain Region: Places and Their Native American Associations* (Bean, Vane, and Young 1981), but it contains approximately twice as much information. It covers more of the Cahuilla territory, and benefits from the fact that in the intervening years we have continued to do research among the Cahuilla, and have added considerably to our knowledge of the Cahuilla landscape, especially in the vicinity of Palm Springs. Particularly useful has been a recent study that has involved the delineation of the *Kauisiktum* and *Paniktum* catchment basin, for which we have depended extensively on the careful location of sites described in the migration stories told by such Cahuilla elders as Alejo Patencio, Francisco Patencio, Akasem Levi, and others, and subsequently published (Patencio 1943, 1971; Strong 1929).

The purpose of the 1981 study was to put together data on the cultural resources of the Santa Rosa Mountains and associated parts of the California desert as part of a larger study then being conducted by the Bureau of Land Management Desert Planning Staff. This larger study was directed toward the identification and evaluation of Native American traditional use areas, ritually associated resource localities, and sacred locations or areas, so that these Native American sites under the jurisdiction of the Bureau of Land Management could be identified, evaluated, and protected. The research results also assisted the Bureau of Land Management to make sure that projects initiated by the Bureau or actions coming under its jurisdiction did not inadvertently harm or destroy cultural resources.

The data in the original study were designed to be used in a desert-wide land use allocation plan for the California Desert Conservation Area, an area even then seriously threatened by the rapidly growing population of southern California. The Study Area included selective locations in the Santa Rosa Planning Units of Riverside County and small portions of San Diego and San Bernardino Counties (see attached maps). Emphasis is placed on vacant public domain within the California desert in and adjoining the Santa Rosa Mountains.

In addition to meeting the above listed objectives, the original study provided considerable new data regarding Cahuilla land use and occupancy, new interpretations of data that had previously been available, and new interpretations of data that were for the first time placed in a unified context. This revised version continues in these directions.

In this revision of the study, we have expanded the Study Area to cover most of the Cahuilla territory, bringing in privately owned lands, U. S. Forest Service lands, and lands set aside as Indian Reservations. These added areas include San Gorgonio Pass, the parts of the Coachella Valley not previously included, and the San Jacinto Mountains. The Cahuilla area that is little represented is the San Jacinto Valley, which was Cahuilla when the Spanish arrived. By the time anthropologists arrived on the scene, most of the Cahuilla inhabitants of this area had died of European diseases, had moved to other places, or had been brought into Mission San Gabriel or other missions, and Luiseños and

1

Serranos had moved into the area. In recent months we have found that the Mission San Gabriel records contain a great deal of information about the Cahuillas of the precontact period. We are presently analyzing these data for publication, and look forward to adding what is appropriate of our findings to some future edition of this work.

We have assembled the information for this study from Cahuilla oral literature, and from both published and unpublished ethnographic literature on the Cahuilla, and to some extent, their neighbors the Serrano and the Chemehuevi. It is not a complete compendium of Cahuilla places. Much of what Cahuillas used to know is now lost. In another respect, it would be impossible to reconstruct the many places and areas the Cahuillas named. They are too numerous to include. For example, Bean acquired for a small area in 1958 dozens of names for "spots"--where a home was, a small hill a mile eastward, or where some notable event had occurred. The Cahuilla area as a whole must have had thousands of place names.

The early scholars who worked with the Cahuilla were not trained linguists. Each developed his or her own system of spelling Cahuilla words. The same place name can therefore appear in a number of guises. Sometimes the same name is spelled in two ways by the same author, even in the course of a page. To make it easier for the reader to refer to sources such as Strong (1929), Gifford (1918), and Patencio (1943), we have used their spellings as given, with the exception that we have capitalized place names, clan names, and lineage names even if they are uncapitalized in the original.

In Chapter IV we have alphabetized descriptions of sites, and commented on their significance, referring when appropriate to discussions in Chapter III. A number given each site refers to its location on our maps. We have alphabetized by the Cahuilla place name used by Patencio (1943) or Strong (1929) wherever possible. Lest this prove a barrier to the convenient use of the alphabetized list by those who know the English placename only, or the Cahuilla word as spelled by someone else, we have prefaced the alphabetized list by a list of equivalent names that will permit the reader to go from the term he or she knows to the term by which we alphabetized.

CULTURAL RESOURCE MANAGEMENT CONCERNS

We can say with some assurance that most of the places described and discussed in this book are considered sacred or historically sensitive by the Cahuilla, that the Cahuilla are concerned about any impact on the sites, and that Cahuillas should be consulted when it appears that a proposed project will have a negative impact on a site or sites. Because so much knowledge has been lost over the past decades during which many traditional persons have passed away, it is difficult to determine the **relative** sensitivity of the various sites, and it may not always be possible to make contact with a representative sample of concerned Native Americans. The authors have interviewed a great many Native Americans with respect to their concern for cultural resources in the course of nearly fourteen years of cultural resource management studies in southern California. Since our summarized findings may be helpful to those readers who are faced with decisions about sensitivity, we are presenting these findings here, in hope that they will be of use in such circumstances:

I.   When we try to decide the relative impact of alternative site use, we give weight to information from the following sources:

1.   Current testimony from the tribal group in whose traditional territory a site lies. Where a site lies in territory held by one or more tribal groups, and the information varies from one to another, special weight is given to those who have most recently lived in or used the area. Regular occupation is given more weight than occasional use. In cases of disagreement that cannot otherwise be resolved, it is judged that the most negative impact should receive special consideration.

2.   Information gathered in the course of recent cultural resource management studies with respect to the expected impact of cultural

resources by such facilities as housing developments, golf courses, dams, transmission lines, generating stations, or pipe lines, and based on consultation with tribal groups whose traditional lands are affected. The remarks about variations in Paragraph 1 would hold in this case as well.

3.   Information from ethnographic, linguistic, historic, archaeological, and other literature--published and unpublished. Especially valuable are the records of tribal groups' oral literature when it is possible to identify places whose Native American names can be equated with present-day names on maps. This kind of literature was usually collected from knowledgeable tribal elders who are now deceased.

II.   We rate the relative impacts of alternative sites use with respect to Native American values on the basis of whether the following conditions are present, and the location and density thereof.

A site is judged very sensitive to impact if it is sacred. Among the kinds of places deemed sacred are:

1.   Sources of residual sacred power, creation sites, and other sites named after or closely identified with powerful sacred persons or happenings. In southern California, these are often mountain tops, but may also be caves, rockshelters, springs (especially hot or mineral), or rock art sites.

A site is also judged very sensitive to impact if it has ritual associations. The following kinds of sites are associated with ritual:

2.   Ritual sites (may often be the same as above), burial and cremation sites; places used for prayer and meditation, for healing, and for training shamans; places where materials (plants, animals, or minerals) for sacred use are gathered.

The presence of ritual objects such as quartz crystals, shamans' bundles, or ground figures indicates that a place is sacred.

Also very sensitive:

4.   Rock art sites are assumed to have had ritual connotations when made, and are considered sacred by most Native Americans. These are particularly vulnerable to impact when anything makes them more accessible.

Sites sensitive to Native Americans because of association with their traditional life:

5.   Native American trails, and places where they are known to have passed in pursuing religious, social, or economic goals, very often all of these at once.

6.   The sites of villages, with the most recent ones most sacred and sensitive because they have a direct historical connection with living people. Modern reservations and other places where today's Native Americans live are also very sensitive.

7.   Collection areas--or micro ecosystems: Stands of plants, such as pinyon trees, mesquite, palm oases, cacti, and plants providing food,

for California Native Americans--and basketry materials are necessary if the art is to be continued. Species that are endangered or whose ecosystems are endangered are of special concern to Native Americans.

8.   Sites frequented by desert tortoises, desert bighorn sheep, and other animals important to Native Americans. Species that are endangered or whose ecosystems are endangered are of special concern to Native Americans.

9.   Springs and other sources of water. As mentioned above, hot springs or springs where healing rites are performed are especially sensitive, having sacred connotations. It is believed that hot springs are connected underground with sources of power, which can be dangerous, but also can be tapped for healing purposes.

10.   Sites named in traditional songs and other literature.

11.   Sites to which people came to trade, visit, recreate, or process foods.

Significant clues to sensitivity include the presence of bedrock mortars and slicks, other groundstone artifacts, scatters of stone flakes, stone circles, stone effigies, and pottery. Rockshelters and caves may have deep deposits of artifactual materials, including burials, shamans' bundles, quartz crystals, etc. All other things being equal, areas with a high density of artifactual materials are more sensitive than those with low density.

We have found that contemporary Native American concerns are apt to be highest in areas which they presently use, or of which they have a direct historical memory (Bean and Vane 1987).

Eīt, Murray Canyon

Singing Cahuilla Bird Songs at a *Malki* Fiesta

***Fat Mel Mo* with San Jacinto and San Gorgonio Peaks in the Background**

Exploring the Site of the *Ahl–wah–hem'–ke* Village, Agua Alta Canyon

Remains of Stone Structure, Rockhouse Canyon

Eng be cha, Fern Canyon--Palm Trees and Ferns Against the Canyon Wall

IV. AN ETHNOGRAPHIC SUMMARY

The Santa Rosa Mountains (including the San Jacinto Range) were occupied when the Spanish arrived in 1769 by various political units of the Takic-speaking Cahuilla people. The Cahuilla were at that time divided into approximately a dozen independent corporate politico-religious kin groups, patrilineal clans. These clans owned large tracts of territory, each of which included several ecological zones. The tracts usually included areas at both higher and lower elevations so that people could take advantage of the wide variety and seasonality of floral and faunal resources (Bean 1972).

Clans were further divided into lineages that were also corporate groups. Each clan was composed of from two or three to a dozen lineages. Each lineage occupied a particular village site, and also owned specific tracts of land within the clan territory for hunting, gathering, and other purposes. In historic times two or more lineages sometimes occupied one village site. Very often a lineage occupied a specific canyon. Thus the *Paniktum* lineage occupied portions of Andreas Canyon south of Palm Springs, and the related *Kauisiktum* occupied Tahquitz Canyon back of that city. On the other hand, Santa Rosa Canyon was occupied by an entire clan in the late nineteenth century.

Cahuilla clans were organized around a hierarchical religious and political structure. Each clan had one or more ceremonial units (an official, a ceremonial house, and a ceremonial bundle). The ceremonial unit served as the symbolic representation of the sociopolitical reality of the group. These units were part of a larger integrative system (ritual congregation) which connected many politically autonomous groups into a wider religious, economic, and political network of cooperative groups (Bean 1972).

The Cahuilla lived for the most part by hunting and gathering, although there is some indication that agricultural techniques were used prior to European contact. The hunting and gathering techniques were sufficiently developed that some authors have suggested that they enjoyed a quasi-agricultural subsistence technology (Lawton and Bean 1968). The Cahuilla had well established political, marriage, and trade relationships with all of their neighbors, being allied with the Gabrielino toward the coast and the Halchidoma on the Colorado River. They intermarried with and traded frequently with the Diegueño , the Luiseño, the Serrano, the Chemehuevi, and even the Mojave and Yuma, from whom they were separated by other tribal groups or by considerable distances and formidable environments.

The first expedition of Europeans to come near the Cahuilla homeland was that led by Spanish army captain Juan Bautista de Anza in 1774-1776. This expedition traveled across the Anza Borrego Desert into Los Coyotes Canyon, and from there into the Los Angeles Basin. By the late 1700s, Cahuillas near the San Juan Capistrano and San Luis Rey Missions had been baptized. By 1809, Cahuillas from the San Gorgonio Pass area, particularly from Whitewater Canyon, are mentioned in Spanish mission records (Bean 1960). From that time on aspects of European culture spread rapidly among the Cahuilla, who of their own initiative seem to have left their home areas to learn such components of European culture as they wished to incorporate into their own culture. By 1819 an *Asistencia* was established at San Bernardino. The Cahuilla and Serrano were closely associated with it. Mission San Gabriel was grazing cattle as far as Palm Springs shortly thereafter (Bean and Mason 1962). Cahuillas from the Warner's Springs area and Los Coyotes were associated with another *Asistencia* at Pala.

By this time some Cahuillas were already speaking Spanish in the Coachella Valley area, and had a keen political awareness of the ways of Spanish-Mexican culture. They began to develop new political and economic strategies with which to deal with the Spanish. They strengthened themselves politically by confederating several clans or remnants of former clans under one leader by the 1840s. Juan Antonio, Antonio Garra, and Chief Cabezon of the desert were among important leaders who led such confederations. The new political strategies ensured the Cahuilla of considerable political control over their area well into the American period. As late as 1860 the Cahuilla outnumbered the Euroamericans in the area. The Cahuilla were clearly in control of most of the area. The situation changed after a smallpox epidemic in 1863 destroyed large numbers of the Cahuilla. At the same time there was an influx of non-Indians into the area as emigrants arrived from the eastern United States and elsewhere (U.S. Census 1860; Phillips 1975; Bean 1972).

Conditions rapidly became worse for the Cahuilla. Their population was decreasing and they were losing many of their traditional lands to outsiders. Their situation became so desperate that it attracted national attention. Investigations of conditions among the Cahuilla and other southern California Indians, and the desire of non-Indian newcomers to stabilize and/or remove Indians from areas which they wished to occupy or use as rangeland led by 1877 to the establishment of Indian reservations throughout the area. These included what is now Morongo Reservation (originally called Potrero, and then Malki), Agua Caliente Reservation, Augustine Reservation, Cabazon Reservation, Torres-Martinez Reservation, Los Coyotes Reservation, Santa Rosa Reservation, Cahuilla Reservation, Ramona Reservation, and the now-terminated Mission Creek Reservation. Governmental interference in Indian Affairs was at first rather slight, but by 1891 the government had established firm political and economic control over most reservations in the area. Nonetheless, traditional leadership patterns persisted, and much of the traditional religious and political system was intact. Cahuilla were still using many of their traditional hunting and gathering areas. As time went on, they began to rely less upon their traditional subsistence techniques, and became more intensively involved in stock raising, agriculture, and wage labor. By the late 1920s many of the Cahuilla were successfully participating in the American economic system. At this time most Cahuillas were resident members of various reservations. These reservations had established their own quite separate socio-cultural system. This system was not unlike that of the older ritual congregation. Various reservations cooperated regularly in socioeconomic and religious activities which provided substantial economic and political benefits to all the Indian groups in the area. Much of the traditional political structure remained, and many traditional rituals were still practiced (Bean 1978).

In the 1930s the great American Depression affected the Cahuillas along with everyone else. Many Cahuillas who still remembered traditional hunting and gathering practices put them to good use to alleviate economic stresses. The resurgence of such traditional practices during the Depression seems to have been an important factor in the maintenance of Cahuilla knowledge of their original territory and the use of its resources for human subsistence (Bean field notes ca 1960).

World War II and changing economic conditions for small farmers, a drought, and many other factors acted in the other direction, contributing to a decrease of Cahuilla interest in traditional ways as well as a decrease in the exposure of non-Indians to these ways. Many young men served in the military forces. Others left the reservation for war-related jobs. Many elders who had maintained traditions died without passing on significant information about their culture.

Fortunately, from the latter part of the 19th century until the 1930s, several anthropologists had visited the area, and collected valuable data about the Cahuilla while Cahuilla who remembered the old ways were still alive. David Prescott Barrows worked among them in the 1890s, publishing as a result an ethnobotany of the Cahuilla which has become a minor classic (Barrows 1900). A. L. Kroeber worked among the Cahuilla early in the 20th century (Kroeber 1907). E. W. Gifford (1918) came just before World War I, and Lucille Hooper (1920) came shortly afterward. William Duncan Strong (1929) and Philip Drucker (1937) followed. Some years later John Peabody Harrington collected information about the Cahuilla (Walsh 1976). After Harrington left, little work was done on the ethnography of the Cahuillas until Lowell John Bean began to work intensively with them in 1959 (Bean 1960; 1972; field notes, ca. 1960).

It is unfortunate that more work was not done, and that so few of the anthropologists who worked with the Cahuilla were interested in reconstructing the precise patterns of traditional land use and occupancy patterns, because we must now rely on archival research and intensive archaeological research to fill in the gaps in our knowledge about how the Cahuilla area was used. Cahuilla in the early part of this century would still have remembered many of these patterns. This is not to say that ethnographic knowledge is not still available, but that it is more difficult to acquire. Another factor that has inhibited data collection in the Cahuilla area is that much of it comprises lands which either were not intensively used after the establishment of reservations, or were not used by Cahuilla who were visited by field ethnographers. Moreover, even when Cahuillas were using some of this area for hunting and gathering and sacred purposes, they often kept the fact secret from investigators in order to discourage relic hunters and non-Indian hunters of game, and of course to preserve their own sense of ethnic identity. It is only in recent years, when the Cahuilla can see that much of this traditional territory is vulnerable to further Euroamerican intrusion, such as that posed by transmission lines, highways, recreational uses and residential development, that they are taking more active interest in recording data on the traditional use patterns of some of their area. Today the Cahuilla are vigorously pursuing the preservation and reconstruction of their history. Such institutions as Malki Museum, the Cupa Cultural Center, and the Agua Caliente Interpretive Center, which is now in the design stage, are a result of this new attitude.

Settlement Pattern

The southeastern part of the Coachella Valley was a major location for Cahuilla Indian settlement at various periods. It is probable that about a thousand years ago the freshwater Lake Cahuilla was about a hundred miles long, occupying the basin now occupied by the Salton Sea. Some of the Cahuilla developed a lacustrine economy and lived especially along the western and northern shores of the lake. The Colorado River, which fed into it at the time, changed its course about 500 years ago and no longer brought water. The lake began to fall when the water lost by evaporation was no longer being replenished. As it fell the Cahuilla moved their villages and changed their patterns of subsistence to meet the changed circumstances (Wilke 1976). In each period the Santa Rosa Mountain range was an extremely attractive environment for them, providing them with the flora and fauna of both the lower, warmer elevations and the higher and cooler ones. Fewer lineages are known from the area to the north, in part at least because people there were drawn into the missions to a greater extent.

Cahuilla villages were generally located in or near the mouth of a canyon or in a valley. They were set up from the floors of canyons and valleys on one side or the other in order to avoid the significant water run-off coming down the canyons during certain periods. Despite this precaution, flash floods that destroyed entire villages are recorded in Cahuilla oral history. The siting of villages off the canyon or valley floors also placed them in the pathway of mountain breezes, which made the living sites more comfortable most of the year. A more significant fact is that these village sites were usually within an optimum distance from various plant and animal food resources at both low and high altitudes. Bean has suggested that most villages whose locations are known had approximately 80 percent of the food resources that people used the year around within a five mile (8 km) radius (1972 :73-74). Elevations above 5000 feet (1.5 km) in most of the Cahuilla area are relatively rare. Places at such heights were used occasionally for specific hunting and gathering activities. Snow and inclement weather, of course, prevented people settling permanently at these heights. In some instances the Cahuilla had winter and summer settlements. We have been told by older Cahuilla informants that in such places as Rockhouse Canyon people would move from village sites at high elevations such as Old Santa Rosa village down to the area of Hidden Springs, *Ataki*, during the colder months to enjoy the warmer climate and to collect the plant foods available there (Bean field notes ca. 1960). Patencio mentions a similar movement among the people in the Palm Springs area (1943).

It is necessary to rely on Mission Records and on ethnographic data collected in earlier years in order to establish in any detail what Cahuilla settlement patterns were before contact. Even when William Duncan Strong worked with them in the 1920s, Cahuilla had moved around a great deal and it was difficult to establish where some of their homes had been at any great distance into the past. Fortunately, Cahuilla oral literature recounts some of the movement of individual lineages in the various clans so that a general pattern over time can be discerned. Cahuillas moved about in response to climatic changes, because of pressures and opportunities derived from Euroamericans, and because of the effects of epidemic diseases introduced by European populations. There was a movement from the areas of Santa Rosa and Los Coyotes canyons eastward. Some of the people in Los Coyotes Canyon moved to Rockhouse Canyon in the middle or late 19th century. Many of the people who had lived in the Santa Rosa area became followers of Juan Antonio (*Costakik* lineage), and moved into the San Timoteo area or the San Gorgonio Pass area. Others moved from the Santa Rosa area out into the Colorado Desert and into the Coachella Valley. The people who moved from Los Coyotes Canyon to Santa Rosa village in Rockhouse Canyon apparently amalgamated to some degree with the Cahuillas of the original clan of that village. They lived there until the late 19th century when most of them moved to the present Santa Rosa Indian Reservation. This move was apparently made because the Cahuilla were beginning to move out more into American society and the reservation provided them with a guaranteed land base, and easier access to jobs and materials they needed to supplement their subsistence.

Other Cahuilla moved a shorter distance into Coachella Valley from villages in *Toro* Canyon, Martinez Canyon, and other canyons on the desert side of the Santa Rosa Mountains. These people maintained hunting and gathering privileges in the area where they had previously lived, as did those who left Los Coyotes and Rockhouse Canyon villages. These traditional hunting and gathering rights were gradually eroded by time and distance. The final *coup de grace* to traditional land use patterns came in the 1890s with the full development of the reservation system. Indian agents and school teachers came in, children were put in Catholic or government boarding schools, and plans for economic development on reservations began to be implemented. There was an increasing hostility on the part of the invading non-Indians toward the idea of Indians using or encroaching upon any lands that were not federally mandated Indian reserves. Descriptions of what happened to Native American economic systems in southern California during and after this period can be found in Bean's discussion of what happened at Morongo reservation (1978) and in Florence Shipek's Ph.D. dissertation (1977).

Springs, Streams and Wells

In an area where rainfall is low, settlements must be placed where there is a dependable water supply. In some places in the desert where ground water was relatively close to the surface, the Cahuilla dug walk-in wells to supply their water needs. In most places they were dependent on either springs or year-round streams. Mesquite groves and palm oases developed where there was water close to the surface. Canyons such as Palm, Andreas, and Murray had year-round streams. Many mountain areas in the Santa Rosa Mountains had springs. It can be assumed that spring sites were places known to the Cahuilla and used by them, and that there were villages or significant use sites near all major springs. Springs and especially hot springs were religiously significant to the Cahuilla, as to their neighbors.

Fauna

Pronghorn sheep, *Antilocarpa americana* (Cahuilla: *tenily*); mountain sheep, *Ovus canadensis* (Cahuilla: *pa?at*); and mule deer, *Odocoileus hemionus* (Cahuilla: *suqat*) were the principal large game animals of the Cahuilla. The fast running pronghorn, popularly known as "antelope," were chased by relays of hunters from the flatlands where they grazed into mountain canyons where they could be boxed into side canyons. In other situations they were chased until they were tired enough to be caught, to be clubbed or shot with bows and arrows (Bean 1972:58).

The mountain sheep were regarded by the Cahuilla as very important animals. They were hunted, according to Cahuilla consultants, in Martinez, *Toro*, Palm, Andreas and other canyons. A mountain sheep, *patem wa ha*, figures in stories of the Cahuilla dream time. The mountain sheep was associated with Orion, a left-handed hunter, and his arrow. Moreover, as a rare and endangered species, the mountain sheep are symbolic representations of the Cahuilla past, and as such are held in virtually reverent esteem. Any place, therefore, where mountain sheep still range, is highly sensitive to the Cahuilla.

The habitat of the mountain sheep was the "high desert scrub country and on the rocky canyon scarps, especially in the pinyon-juniper life zone. In colder seasons they moved into the Lower Sonoran areas to feed on the various desert plants" (Bean 1972:57). Patencio says that wild mountain sheep go to the top of Murray Peak at lambing time (1943:71). Here where it was warm and sunny on the slopes of this high hill, the rams could keep a lookout for danger all about the high country. The lambing season was in summer, ending by mid-August. There were herds in San Gorgonio Pass, in Whitewater Canyon, in Palm Springs and as far south as the Borrego Desert, some on the desert slopes of the Santa Rosa Mountains in Riverside and San Diego counties. Their preferred habitat was between 800 and 4000 feet (240-1200 m) elevation, below the pinyon-juniper belt. This was the habitat of agaves, Opuntia cacti, yucca and scrub oak. They browsed the rocky slopes of such areas, wherever there was the water they needed for survival.

Mountain sheep were hunted for food, for sinew for bows, and for their skins. The mule deer during most of the year were found in "open forested areas and meadows, and in the winter. . . the chaparral-covered slopes and rocky canyons" (1972:57). They would have been found in spring, summer and fall in the upper Santa Rosa Mountains--in Pinyon Flat, Little Pinyon Flat, and Pinyon Flat Alta, for example. In winter they came down the canyons, and could be found in small herds of six to ten in willow and cottonwood thickets. The mule deer were also symbolically important to the Cahuilla. It was considered very important that the appropriate rituals associated with deer hunting be properly carried out. Mountain lions were sacred, and were not hunted. Eagles, hawks, and other birds of prey were sacred. Eagles figured prominently in ceremonial events. The small game animals were significant staples in the Cahuilla diet--rabbits, squirrels, chipmunks, rats and mice being regularly hunted and eaten. Communal rabbit hunts were often organized before ceremonial events to provide food for guests. Calistro Tortes asserted that there is a place worn smooth like concrete in Rockhouse Canyon where they chased and caught rabbits (Bean field notes ca. 1960). The species of rabbit which were found in the Cahuilla homeland were *Lepis californicus* (Cahuilla: *su?is*), the blacktailed jack rabbit; *Sylvilagus audubonii* (Cahuilla: *tavut*), the desert cottontail (Bean 1972:59). Woodrats were common throughout the Cahuilla area. Informants mentioned specifically places such as Deep Canyon, *Toro* and Santa Rosa peaks, and coniferous forests on canyon slopes. The woodrats travel as high as 2000 feet (600 m), and flourish in "oak woodland, chaparral, rocky cactus areas and creosote bush habitats" (Bean 1972:59). These were prized as food by the Cahuillas. Their habitats being conspicuous, they are frequently vandalized. They should be protected by advising people using the area to protect and not destroy them.

Desert tortoises were used as food and their shells as ritual and household containers. They are primarily found near dunes and washes, near plant clusters and in rocky areas. The shell was used as a rattle--a musical instrument used in ceremonies. Desert tortoises are active in the daytime during spring, summer and fall, and sometimes at night during the summer. In areas where vehicular use is common, people should be warned that these animals, wherever they occur, should be protected. Their destruction has been a matter of considerable anxiety to Cahuilla, an anxiety that has been expressed in ethnographic notes for many years.

Rocks

Rocks were often named by the Cahuilla. They were often used as places to store food and goods. Others were sacred places where religious acts were performed and supernatural power acquired. Any large or unusual formation of rock was apt to be considered sacred. Some of these are identified in this report. Wherever there are known sacred rocks or unusual rocks which might be sacred, they should not be placed in jeopardy by construction or recreational use of the area. Wherever rock caves are found, they should be protected if possible.

The Naming of Sites

Some Cahuillas state that all places were given names by their people. The Cahuilla developed a sophisticated taxonomic system for geographical features which could precisely describe a geographic phenomenon. One of the reasons given for this was that having names or precise designations for most places made it easier for hunters or gatherers to know where they were so that they could return themselves, or send out other people to an area where a kill had been made or a botanical or mineral resource found. The hunter or collector could leave whatever game or other resource he could not or did not carry home, and anyone he sent out could find it without any difficulty (Bean field notes ca. 1960).

In addition to names for specific places, the Cahuilla had generalized place names. For example, the word for dividing line or boundary was *Keywatwahhewena* (Patencio 1971: 56-57). According to Alice Lopez, the word for a place to camp for the night, as in "I am going to sleep here tonight," was *tuka*; a place where no one lives, an uninhabited or wild area, was called *iikinga*; a place where you sit down, a temporary place, was called *chemnachvayika*; and the name for a place where people live was *pachemkalivay*. The term *hemki* generally meant home, a place where people live, and the term *pahemnach* meant people travelling around.

The Cahuillas tended to name every spring, conspicuous rock, major outcrop of rock, canyon, grove, or other geographic manifestations in their area. Place names often translate into terms describing the environment, such as "near the mouth," "in a canyon," "by the spring," "place of the acorn trees," "place of the palm trees," "place of grass seeds," and so on. One village even had a name referring to the fact that there was cracked earth there--the San Andreas fault passed through it. Another clan's name translates "touched by the river," a name which suggests that the clan came from a place which had experienced a flash flood.

Giving names to all parts of the environment is consistent with the general Cahuilla view of the world, which holds that humans, plants, animals, and all other natural elements were merged into one single consistent and interdependent whole, and that often these independent parts are reservoirs of residual "power" or symbolic representations of personages of the Cahuilla creation time that could still affect the daily lives of people (Bean 1976).

Oral Literature

Many of the features in Cahuilla ethnography are explained in Cahuilla myths and legends. Cahuilla oral literature has not been as extensively recorded as one might hope, nor has linguistic investigation been complete, so we will probably never have the complete semantic domain of that subject that resided in the minds of tribal historians in the past. However, what has been recorded, such as that by Patencio (1943; 1971), Gifford (1918), Kroeber (1908; 1925), and Seiler (1970) does give us a strong indication of the detail with which physiographic features were recorded. For example, rock indentations left by *nukatem*, in *illo tempore*, that is, creation time, where culture heroes walked or leaned or sat, are mentioned. It is generally thought by Cahuillas that every adult Cahuilla knew with considerable precision the areas that belonged to him or were used by his family, his lineage, and even his clan. Certainly they knew where tribal group boundaries were, and knew a considerable amount of anecdotal material, both historic and mythic, about each of these places. The older Cahuillas interviewed in the 1960s took considerable pride about the detail with which they could remember geographic features and names of many of them. These names served as devices for stimulating traditional stories about Cahuilla culture and history.

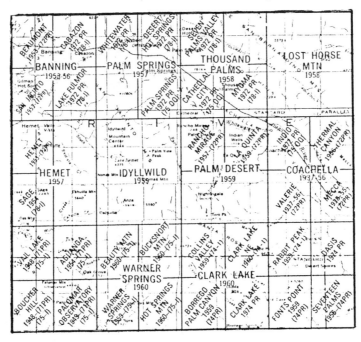

Guide to Maps in Next Chapter

V. CAHUILLA REGIONS

Several areas in the San Jacinto and Santa Rosa Mountain regions were centers of occupation and must be discussed in some detail because of the great concern that Cahuillas have for these areas.

San Gorgonio Pass and Whitewater Canyon

The Canyons which drained into the San Gorgonio Pass and their associated flat lands were the territory of various lineages of the *Wanakik* Cahuilla clan, mistakenly identified by Kroeber (1908), Gifford (1918), and Benedict (1924) as Serrano. Strong (1929), and Bean (1960), who benefitted from more extensive fieldwork, found that they were Cahuilla who spoke a slightly different dialect than the Cahuillas to the south and west. Bean identified ten different lineages: the *Ackit Wanakik* in the Canyon area north of present-day Beaumont; the *Pisata Wanakik* in Banning Water Canyon, *Pīhatapa* (176); the *Waksishe Wanakik* near Cabezon; the *Palukna Wanakik* in Stubbe Canyon (160); the *Wanakik Wanakik* in Whitewater Canyon (272); the *Teshana Wanakik* at Snow Creek (128); the *Wakina Wanakik* at Blaisdell Canyon (271); the *Haviña Wanakik* at Palm Springs Station (63); the *Huvana Wanakik* at Hall's Grade (73); and the *Amnaa Vitcem* at an unidentified place northwest of Palm Springs (1960). Of these lineages, the *Wanakik* lineage was the *ʔa čaʔi*, or "first" lineage, whose *net* was the nominal leader of all the *Wanakik* lineages (Bean 1960; 1972:87).

Whitewater Canyon (272) was the home territory of the *Wanakik* lineage, a favored wintering home of many of the *Wanakik* people, according to Bean's informant, Victoria Wierick (Bean field notes ca. 1960). The families living there moved away sometime late in the 1800s after a flash flood destroyed the main village site. They moved to *Malki* (116), sometimes referred to as Potrero, or Genio's Village. This is now the Morongo Reservation. Descendants of the *Wanakik Wanakik* lineage include the Pablo family at Morongo Reservation.

The Cahuilla name of the Whitewater Canyon village site was *Wanup* (272) (Benedict 1924:112; Bean 1960:112).

To the east of Whitewater Canyon is an area called Devil's Garden (42). This is an area where many different kinds of cactus grow, and was traditionally an important food gathering place for the *Wanakik* Cahuilla, and in recent years for many others. Barrel cacti are plentiful there. This species was a primary food resource for the Cahuilla, particularly in the spring months (See Bean and Saubel 1972:67-68).

Cottonwood Canyon (32) was also an important food collecting and gathering site for Cahuilla Indians. Several archaeological sites have been reported in the area. Indigenous plant and animal food resources in this area are numerous, as they are throughout this part of the secondary study area. There are significant trails crisscrossing this area (Johnston 1960).

Kawishmu (94) was recorded by Kroeber as the name of "a small hill east of White Water, marking the boundary between the *Wanupiapayum* and the desert Cahuilla" (1908).

Franciso Patencio says that the Cahuilla culture hero, *Evon ga net*, marking boundaries for "new tribes to come, crossed the desert from Eagle Canyon (51) to the north, and turned west along the Whitewater River wash." He found desert willows growing along Whitewater Wash, and called the place *Con kish wi qual (31)*, which means "two desert willows." Then he went south across the valley to where jagged red rocks "still stand alone by the side of the highway." He named these *Kish*

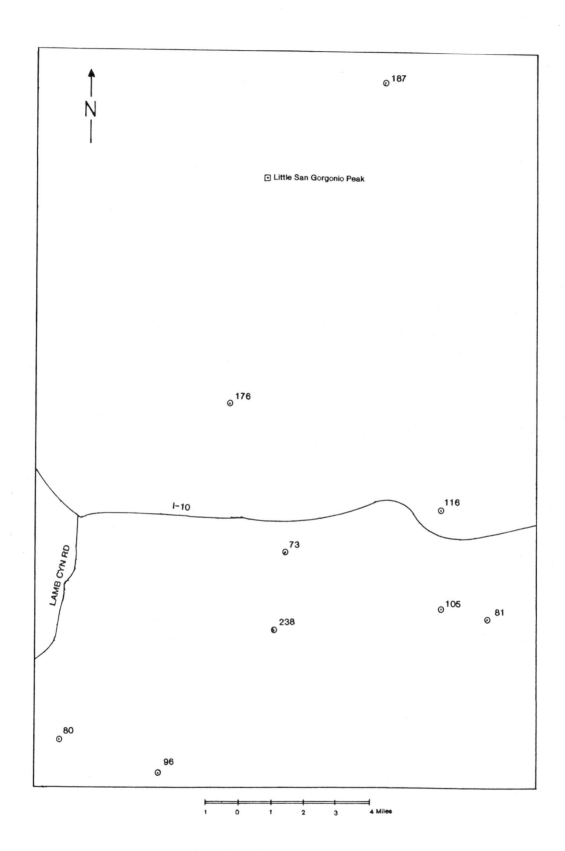

⊙ 187

☐ Little San Gorgonio Peak

⊙ 176

I-10

⊙ 116

LAMB CYN RD

⊙ 73

⊙ 105

⊙ 81

⊙ 238

⊙ 80

⊙ 96

1 0 1 2 3 4 Miles

Map of Portion of the San Gorgonio Region
Based on the
Banning, California Quadrangle, 15-minute series, USGS Topographic Map

chowl (100), "sharp pointed house roofs." Three quarters of a mile along the Whitewater "ditch," he named a large pile of rocks *Lin Kish mo.* "Going west along the valley, which is now the highway, he came to another point. This he called *Ta was ah mo,* meaning a good view for hunting." Going on, he called Whitewater Point *Ta mare* (219), meaning the mouth or opening of a pass, crossed Snow Creek and named it *Na hal log wen et* (128), "the center of an open place." He next came to a spring at a point that he called *E va we* (52), the "wind blows all the time." At the end of his journey he passed into a mountain and came out as a great white dome on the top that can be seen from Whitewater to Cabezon--*Kow wish so kalet* (105), the rock sign in which *Evon ga net,* the fox, still lives (Patencio 1943:54).

The Palm Springs Area

The city of Palm Springs developed around the hot springs, *Sec he* (203), called Agua Caliente by the Spanish. These were also a center of Cahuilla occupation and religious activity. There are numerous references in the literature to these springs. They belonged to the Kauisiktum lineage, whose territory embraced Tahquitz (26) and Chino (114) Canyons and the surrounding area.

Kauisiktum **Territory**

The *Kauisiktum* and the *Paniktum* are lineages that, with the *Acitcem,* belonged to a clan whose name has not been preserved. The *Acitcem* belonged to the Coyote moiety, and the other two to the Wildcat moiety. The *Acitcem* originally lived in Palm Canyon, but gave it to the *Kauisiktum,* with whom they had intermarried, and moved to Indian Wells at some time in the past (Strong 1929:91). In the 1870s, the Agua Caliente Indian Reservation was established for them. The reservation included *Sec he,* the hot springs, which proved a magnet for non-Indians seeking a desert climate in which to recover from pulmonary and other ailments. The Indian/non-Indian village that has grown up from a village whose phone book could be listed on two pages as late as 1930 is now the world famous resort of Palm Springs.

The extent of the traditional territory of the *Kauisiktum* lineage is known in greater detail than that of any other Cahuilla lineage because two different lineage leaders left their versions of Cahuilla migration stories. Alejo Patencio gave Strong an account of the "great *net's* travels laying out the boundaries of his people's territory (1929:100-101). About two decades later his brother Francisco Patencio told Margaret Boynton stories of the travels of *Evon ga net* and of a later head man, *Ca wis ke on ca.* These accounts appeared in Patencio's *Stories and Legends of the Palm Springs Indians* (1943). A careful reading of Strong's account reveals that one of the three names with which the "great *net*" starts out is "Kauiskiauka," which is clearly another spelling for "Ca wis ke on ca." When the great *net* arrives at the *Iva,* a hot springs north of Soboba, one of the two new names he assumes is "Ivañanet," a name that could also be spelled "*Evon ga net.*" The stories of the three, as given, are similar in general, but vary in details. The great *net* started with his people at Redland Junction, and takes them in turn to or past *Iva* (80), *Kekliva* (96), *Aīakaīc (San Jacinto Peak)* (6), *Panyik (the mouth of Andreas canyon)* (10), *Milyillilikalet* (123), *Tekic* (10), *Sēwitckul (Murray Hill)* (207), *Ēit* (48), *Palhilikwinut* (145), *Tēvin' imulwiwaīnut* (242), *Paskwa* (165), *Tatmīlmī (at south end of Palm Canyon)* (165), *Sewī* (206), *Sīmūta* (210), *Pīnalata* (177), *Kalahal* (87), *Tchial* (225), *Kaukwicheki* (91), *Pūlūkla* (183), *Aīakaic* (6), *Yauahic* (282) (just south of Blaisdell Canyon), the latter the northwestern limit of his territory (Strong 1929:100-101). He then went southeast from Murray Hill (207) to *Taupakic* (221), *Konkistū-uinut* (103), and *Alhauik* (9) (possibly Indio Mountain). From the mouth of Andreas Canyon, he named in turn *Kauissimtcem hempkī* (89), *Temukval* (235), *Tekelkukuaka* (228), *Kakwawit* (86) (mouth of Tahquitz Canyon), *Kauiskī* (88), *Mīaskalet* (122), *Palhanikalet* (144), *Iñvitca* (99), *Tepal* (138), *Tūīval* (246), *Tetcavī* (240), *Pūlūvil* (184) ("the large smooth rock cliff at Dry Falls"), *Kauistanalmū* (90), *Havīñen* (61), *Hauītalal* (62), *Waīvas* (270), *Malal* (115), *Kistcavel* (100), *Pīonvil* (172), *Teūamal* (241), *Tama* (219), *Awelmū* (13), *Niñkicmū* (134), *Paklic* (142), and finally, a sharp hill south of Cabezon, *Ivawakik* (81) (Strong 1929:100-101).

Evon ga net and his people were at Moreno (289) when he started his trip to mark boundary

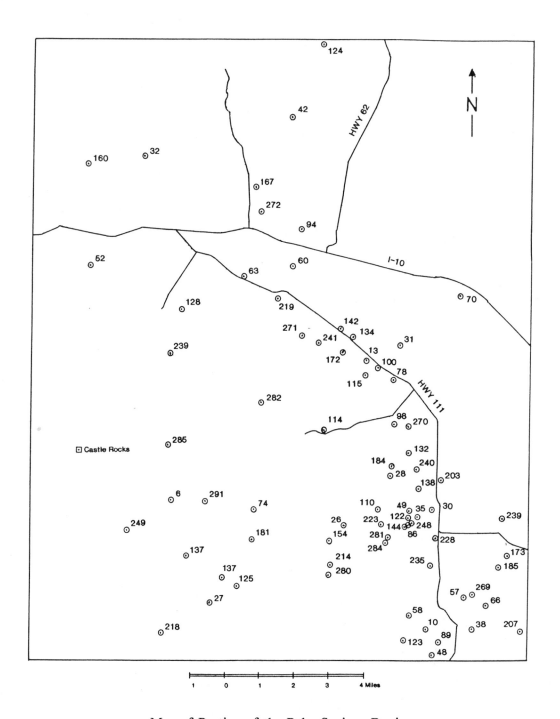

Map of Portion of the Palm Springs Region
Based on the
Palm Springs, California 1957 Quadrangle, 15-minute series, USGS Topographic Map

lines. He went in turn to Gilman's Hot Springs (81), Mount San Jacinto (6), *To quo a* (249), *Pul lo cla* (183) (a rock on Tahquitz Peak), *Cow qhish hec i*, *Sung pa* (215), *Tep po we* (237), *Sim mo ta* (210) (in Palm Canyon), *Fat mel mo* (53), *Gash mo* (57) (east of the Garden of Eden), *Cow wis to lek ets* (38), *Wa wash ca le it* (269) (Murray Hills), *Qua al hec ik* (185), *Pe ya hot mor am mah* (173) (Song Point), *I was wa ba all* (83), *E pah* (51) (Eagle Canyon and Springs), *Ca wish is mal* (23) (Cathedral Canyon), *Pa ute em* (171), *Soungle, Con kish we qual* (31), *Kish chowl* (100), *Lin Kish mo* (rocks in Whitewater ditch), *Pe on bel* (172), *Ta was ah mo, Ta mare* (219) (Whitewater Point), *Na hal log wen et* (128) (Snow Creek), *E va we* (52), and finally, a dome on top of a mountain that can be seen from Whitewater to Cabazon, *Kow wish so kalet* (105) (Patencio 1943:52-54).

Francisco Patencio says that the Fox Tribe, *Evon ga net's* people, settled down in canyon country near Soboba Hot Springs. The head man *Ca wis ke on ca*, traveling about the country, recognized the places marked for his people by *Evon ga net*, including *Pow ool* (181) (Hidden Lake) and *Sec he* (203) (Agua caliente), but the country was occupied by the *Mu na lem*, who belonged to the *Ha ve* people of Seven Palms, with whom the Fox People had to do battle to get possession of the *Sec he* area. Later *Ca wis ke on ca's* people and those of his clan brother *Mum on quish* attacked Seven Palms, and carried the heads of the slain to Palm Canyon, where they broke them against a rock at *You koo hul ya me* (283) (Patencio 1943:85-89).

Three brothers descended from *Ca wis ke on ca* headed new lineages. One brother established himself first at *Chow o hut* (28) (Little Tachevah), then at *Cock wo wit* (30) across Tahquitz Canyon, and finally at *Tev ing el we wy wen it* (242) at the mouth of Palm Canyon. The youngest brother moved first to *Yum ich you* (286) (Thousand Palms Canyon), and then down the valley to *Sawit ha push* (202), known as the Snake's Eye (Patencio 1943:90-91).

Ca wis ke on ca went up Chino Canyon and marked the rock near the top of the mountain *Tahquitz wayo ne va* (218). In succession he named *Chis hill mo* (27), *Poo ool* (181) (Hidden Lake), *Hoon wat hec ic, Mow it check mow win it* (291), *Young ga vet wit ham pah va* (285), *Ow kee ve lem* (137), *Mum yum muck ca* (125), *Woh hut cli a low win it* (280), *Pal pis o wit* (154) (spring on the south of Tahquitz Canyon), *Sum mat chee ah wen e* (214), *Chee mo ke wen e* (26) (Tahquitz Canyon), *Ta vish mo* (223), *Yan heck e* (281), *You ye va al* (284), *Tong wen nev al* (248), *Me ahs cal et* (122), *Eng be cha* (49), *Pa cale* (138), *To e ve val* (246), *Ng natches pie ah* (132), *Ta che va* (184), *Key wat wah he wen e* (98), *Num na sh b al* (135), *Ish el wat tow ta um ali* (48), *Mes al em* (114) (plant in Chino Canyon), *Pa hal ke on a* (139), *Hou wit s sa ke* (72), *Hoon wit ten ca va* (70) (Garnet Hills), *Kick ke san lem mo* (99), *Tem ma ves el* (234), *Tak el ko ko a ka* (228), and finally back to his home in Palm Springs (Patencio 1943:95-99).

These places are identified, insofar as possible, in the alphabetical listing.

Palm Canyon (228)

This canyon is said by tradition to have belonged originally to the *Atcitem* lineage, and to have been given by them to the *Kauisiktum* lineage, to whom they were related by marriage. Because *Kauisiktum* leaders recorded much of their oral literature, there is a considerable amount of data about their traditional areas. Palm Canyon is conspicuous because of its splendid natural resources, inspiring suggestions that it be developed as a private or public recreational area, such as a National Park. As a result of tribal opposition to this idea, the canyon remains in a relatively pristine condition.

Cahuilla oral history of the canyon includes the story of an early people who walked across the mountains to Palm Canyon from the area of the San Jacinto plain. One of their leaders turned himself into a rock and "he is there in the rock yet" (Patencio 1943:33). This is now one of the many "power" rocks in Cahuilla territory. Any large rock formation in the Cahuilla area is likely to be such a transformed personage, or a place of residual supernatural power from the Cahuilla "beginnings."

In another account the son of *Ca wis ke on ca*, an important culture hero, moved to Palm Canyon from a previous home (Patencio 1943:90). Another culture hero, *Evon ga net*, called a place in Palm Canyon *Sim mo ta* (210) meaning "Indian corral or pasture." He named a second place in the

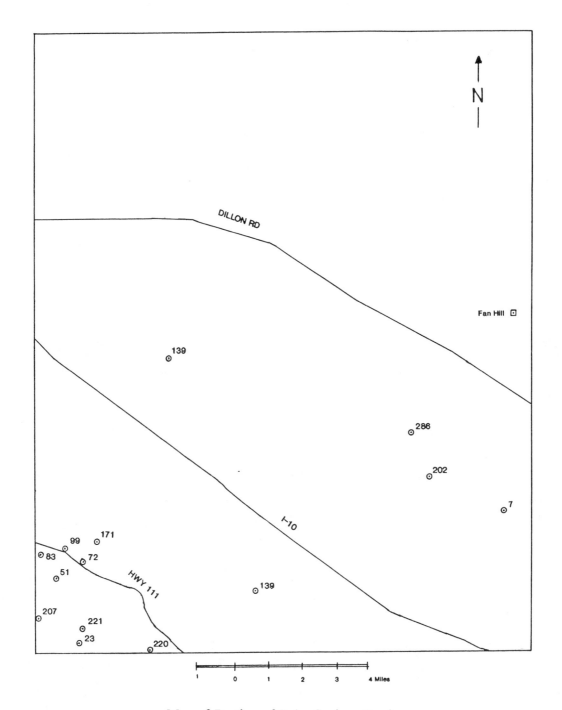

Map of Portion of Palm Springs Region
Based on the
Thousand Palms, California 1957 15-minute Series, USGS Topographic Map

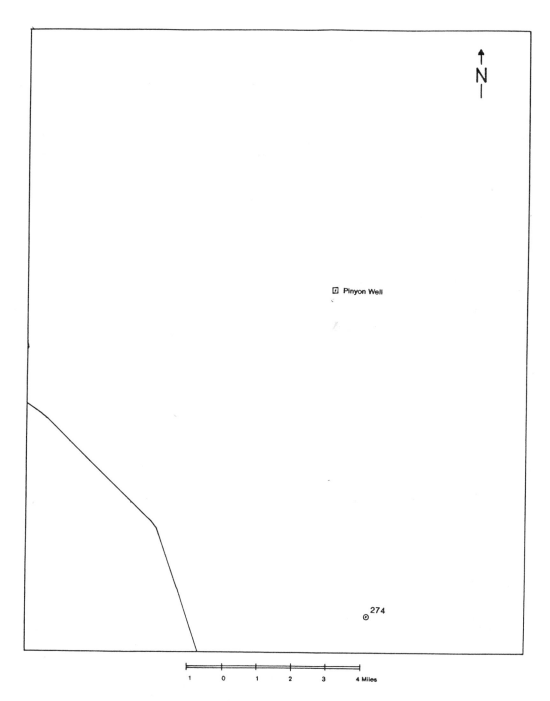

Map Showing Homeland of the Wavaaikiktum
Based on the
Lost Horse Mtn. 1959 Quadrangle, 15-minute Series, USGS Topographic Map

canyon *Fat mel mo* (53), meaning "a place along many hills". A third place named by the culture hero, *Gash mo* (57), meaning "the sound of crunching sand as one walks," is said to be a place to the east side of the area once called the "Garden of Eden" (Patencio 1943:53).

The son of *Ca wis ke on ca* who moved to a place near Palm Canyon called the place *Tev ing el we wy wen it* (242), meaning "a round flat basket closed up at the top, that is hung up." Here he lived, and raised a family. He had a ceremonial house here. A territory was given him by his brother--the land from "Idyllwild down to Palm Canyon, through the west side of the Murray Hills; then across to the Little Canyon of one Palm near the beginning of the Andreas Club Road, north on Andreas Canyon" (Patencio 1943:90). This may be the description of a lineage's territory, possibly the *Kauisiktum*.

At a place that is now known as Indian Potrero (210), Palm Springs people of the early time are said to have beaten the heads of their Seven Palms enemies on a big rock after a battle between the Palm Springs people and the Seven Palms people. The name of the place *You koo hul ya me* (283) means "place of many brains" (Patencio 1943:89). It appears that the Seven Palms people were displaced by the group that came from the San Jacinto plain area. The presence of petroglyphs in the area signifies the territorial claims of one group over the other.

In another Cahuilla source, William Pablo, *Wanakik* leader, recalls that in 1825 a terrible epidemic of smallpox threatened the Cahuilla people. Indian doctors, he reports, held a council to decide how to treat the disease. The meeting took place in Palm Canyon. In this account the name of Palm Canyon is said to have been "Taquitz." An error of some sort has possibly come through in the translation. This rather lengthy account points out that "paintings and hieroglyphics are found in our Indian caves," which interpret or tell what happened to these caves. Other local personages mentioned in this account include Chief Andres Lucero, presumably of the Andreas family (*Panikiktum* lineage). Sick people were sent to a cave in Chino Canyon to receive treatment and to be "rendered immune" to the disease (Romero 1954:2-4).

At the mouth of Palm Canyon there is a flat rock with mortar holes. The place was called *tēvin' imulwiwaīwinut* (242) (Strong 1929:100). Such places were used for grinding various plant foods by Cahuilla women. They were usually owned by individuals or families (Bean 1972).

Merriam (Field notes, date unknown) says that Palm Canyon was the boundary between two Cahuilla linguistic groups. He interviewed Cahuilla about place names and was given the following data:

The *Paniktem* occupied the lower end of Palm Canyon between the *Kavisik* and the *Wak-ko-chim*. In another note he says that the *Paniktum* were a tribe who occupied the middle part of Palm Canyon, including Murray and West canyons. In still another note he says the *Paniktem* were "over" Palm Canyon, west to Andreas Canyon and up to West Fork Canyon. There was a group called the *Kutam*, one of the *Kavic* group.

Merriam also notes that the *Wak-ko-chim-kut-em* was a "tribe" in the upper part of Palm Canyon--reaching southerly and easterly over Haystack and Asbestos mountains, and Pinyon Flat to the south side of the Santa Rosa mountains (Merriam field notes, undated).

In another place he says that the *Wah-ko-chimut* were around the West Fork to Vandeventer Flat to the base of the Santa Rosa mountains, and down each side of Palm Canyon to opposite West Fork again southeast of the Indian Wells tribe.

Elsewhere he says, "Adjoining the *Wah'-ne-ke'-tem* [*Mahl-ke*] on the southeast are the *Kah'-wis-se-tum* [*Kauisiktum*] or Palm Springs . . . tribe, which begins at the point of the mountain near Whitewater Station and reaches easterly to a huge elongate sand dune (over a rocky base) called *Yah'-wah-kis*; and thence southerly to the mouth of Palm Canyon; across this to the west and up the north rim of San Andreas Canyon to Eagle Cliff at the summit; thence northerly around the head of Tahquitz Canyon and San Jacinto Peak and down the ridge to the place of beginning near Whitewater Station.

"Adjoining the *Kah'-wis-se-tem* on the south are the *Pahn-vik-tem* or Palm Canyon people (*Paniktum*). Their territory embraces Palm Canyon and the adjacent mountain slopes on the west

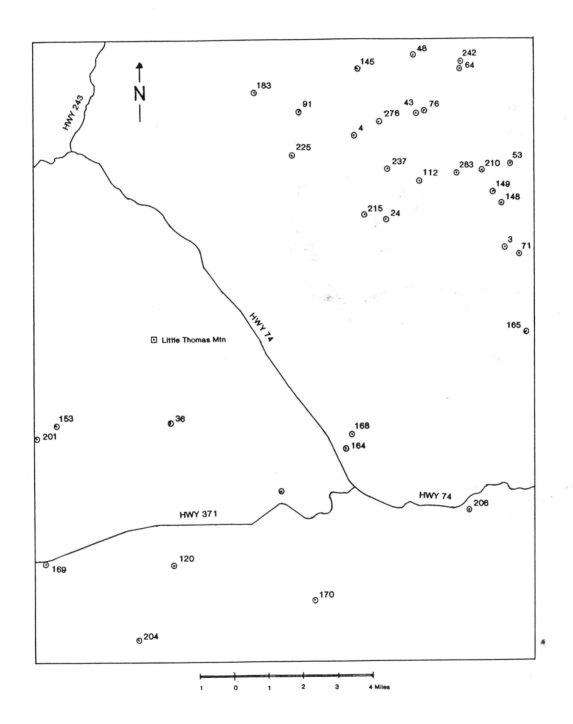

Map of Portion of Palm Springs and Santa Rosa Mountain Regions
Based on the
Idyllwild, California, 1959 15-minute Series, USGS Topographic Map

from the north side of Andreas Canyon to West Fork Canyon.

"Adjoining the *Pahn-vik-tem* on the south were the *Wah-ke-chi'm-kut*, now extinct, who extended southerly over the upper reaches of Palm Canyon and adjacent slopes on both sides from West Fork Canyon to beyond Vandeventer Flat and on to the very base of Santa Rosa Mountain. They spoke the same dialect as the Santa Rosa Mountain people.

"Adjoining the *Wah-ke-chi'm-kut* on the east were the *Kah-vi'-nish* or Indian Wells tribe" (Merriam field notes, date unknown).

Some descendants of the Serranos also have an interest in Palm Canyon. The Serrano at Morongo Reservation were a part of the ceremonial network (ritual congregation) of the people in Palm Springs, as were the peoples at Cahuilla, Santa Rosa, Torres-Martinez and several other reservations of this area. All of these people intermarried, and so are often closely related genealogically. It has been said that the great great grandfather of Sarah Martin, past ceremonial leader of the *Maringa* Serrano, lived for a time in Palm Canyon (Bean field notes ca. 1960). Her great grandmother lived there with him and his wife.

One of the many archaeological features in Palm Canyon was witnessed by desert reporter Randall Henderson, who saw a series of Indian shrines, piles of pebbles and small rocks, spread along both sides of the trail up Palm Canyon at irregular intervals. At the time they were well preserved and quite conspicuous (Henderson 1941).

Palm Canyon stretches southward through the Santa Rosa mountains all the way to Vandeventer Flat. The trail through the canyon was an important link in a complex of trails over which people moved all over southern California. At Vandeventer Flat and elsewhere, it connected with trails that led to Pinyon Flat, Santa Rosa village, and westward to the coast (Patencio 1943:71; Jaeger 1953).

Springs are essential to travellers along any trail in this dry country. There were a number of these along the main trail in Palm Canyon. One of these was Agua Bonita Spring (3), near Big Falls, famous to local travellers. Halfway up the canyon was a hot spring. This spring was named *Paskwa* (165) (means "mortars") by the culture hero, the "great *net*." It was associated with rock mortars (Strong 1929:100). The same *net* named the southern end of Palm Canyon *Tatmilmi* (165) (1929:100). Hermit's Bench Oasis (64), at the lower end of Palm Canyon, is one of many palm oases in the canyon (Henderson 1941:26).

Andreas Canyon

Andreas Canyon branches off from Palm Canyon near its mouth. It has cultural and historical significance to both Indians and non-Indians interested in the area. Its great natural beauty and its cultural significance have drawn the attention of many of those who have been concerned with explaining the southern California desert's positive features to others, such as James (1908; 1918), Chase (1919), Saunders (1913; 1914), and Jaeger (1953).

The mouth of Andreas Canyon provided a home for the Andreas family who made up the Paniktum lineage. By the last half of the nineteenth century they were farming there, and may have farmed there prehistorically. The lineage was headed by Captain Andreas, who died in the early 1880s. Captain Andreas lived in one of several adobe houses in the southwest corner of Section 35, Township 4 S., Range 4 E., S.B.M., but the main part of the settlement was in Section 2, Township 5 S., Range 4 E., S.B.M., directly to the south. *Paniktum hemki: A Study of Cahuilla Cultural Resources in Andreas and Murray Canyons* (CSRI 1983) gives a full account of Andreas Canyon ethnography and ethnohistory, and the results of an archaeological survey of the Canyon mouth.

The territory of the *Paniktum* (Cahuilla), according to Merriam (Field notes, date unknown) was from the north side of Andreas Canyon to the West Fork of Palm Canyon.

Conspicuous archaeological features of the canyon include:

1) A pictograph site, *Tekic* (10) (Patencio 1943:103).

2) A large cave shelter consisting of an over hanging rock under which are bedrock mortars. This is referred to by local people as "Gossip Rock," and by Cahuilla as *Milyillikalet* (123) (Strong 1929:101). Cahuillas have indicated that each grinding rock belonged to a particular family. Most

of these were "washed" away before 1948. Various seeds (acorns, mesquite beans, palm dates) of indigenous plants as well as of domesticated plants were ground in these mortars (Bean field notes ca. 1960).

3) Beneath the rock containing the petroglyph there is a rock with "saw teeth" which was used to draw hide through in order to make it pliable enough for carrying straps, thongs, and the like. This same sheltered area was used to chip arrowheads (Bean field notes ca. 1960).

According to one Cahuilla elder, the pictographs on a rock at the mouth of Andreas Canyon depict the history of the Agua Caliente people, including the "legend of the Palo Verde tree." According to this legend, the great chief *Tachevah*'s daughter was abducted by *Tahquitz*, disappearing at the mouth of Andreas Canyon, where later a Palo Verde tree grew to mark the spot (Klein, date unknown).

Andreas Canyon provided water from several sources for the Cahuilla people living at Rincon. In historic times they brought water in ditches from Andreas Canyon to the groves of figs, grapes, oranges and other plants which they cultivated. Eventually developer B. B. Barney acquired Section 35, and diverted the water from Andreas canyon to his own development, called the "Garden of Eden." George Wharton James (1918:294) recalls that Captain Andreas, who farmed here, was a man of "considerable energy, who lived in an adobe house. He had a vineyard and produced wine for local distribution."

There are several groves of palm trees in the canyon.

The village in Andreas Canyon (10) lay in the area through which one now drives after one buys a ticket to see the Indian Canyons.

The condition of Andreas Canyon in the early part of the century has been described by J. Smeaton Chase in his California Desert Trails (1919). He camped at the rock shelter for several months while journeying through the southern California deserts. The cavern (rock shelter) served as his "dining room, study and kitchen." It was "adorned" by "picture writing." He says an "upper story was quite a museum of age-dimmed records in red and black." He says that one upright stone was "worn into grooves like knuckles, where arrow shafts had been smoothed," and describes a stone that "showed evidence of having been used for polishing the obsidian points." He says a "dozen" bedrock mortars were there, and that occasionally he "unearthed. . .deer-horn awls and ornaments of shell and clay" and various bone materials of different shapes (1919:20).

Jane Penn of Morongo Indian Reservation recalls visiting the canyon at about 1917. Some of the people were still using traditional houses for shelter, and waters were diverted from the stream to the houses for domestic use. Mrs. Penn's father, William Pablo, a well-known political and religious leader of the *Wanikik*, is said to have been born there. Andres *Painik* (Chief Andres) was his maternal grandfather. Andres was born about 1800 at *Painik* near Andreas Canyon (Curtis 1926 :110, photo 2).

The *Kauisiktum* owned a portion of Andreas Canyon, too. According to Merriam (Field notes, date unknown) their territory "begins at the point of the mountain near Whitewater Station and reaches easterly to a huge elongate sand dune (over a rocky base) called *Yah-wah-kis*; and thence southerly to the mouth of Palm Canyon; across this to the west and up the north rim of San Andreas Canyon to Eagle Cliff at the summit; thence northerly around the head of *Tahquitz* Canyon and San Jacinto Peak and down the ridge to the place of beginning near Whitewater Station."

Andreas Canyon also has historic import because Carl Eytel, a famous painter and illustrator, used features of the canyon for much of his art and because the famous pioneer ethnographer and photographer Edward Curtis used the canyon as background for some of his photographic studies of Indian culture.

Andreas Canyon, including the site of Rincon village, is on the National Register of Historic Places.

Ēit (**Murray Canyon**) (48)

This canyon opens into Palm Canyon somewhat to the south of the mouth of Andreas Canyon.

The canyon and its environs are mentioned frequently in Cahuilla oral literature. Francisco Patencio recalled that the Murray Hills are "full of trails," and that wild mountain sheep went to the top of Murray Peak at lambing time. Trails cross the Murray Hills from the "Garden of Eden," passing Eagle Spring (51) on the way to Indian Wells (34), Magnesia Canyon (140), and Cathedral Canyon (23). These run back into Palm Canyon country, joining a trail network that goes to Pinyon Flats and other places of importance in the Santa Rosa mountains (1971:16).

Murray Hill was called *sewitckul* (207), a name given it by the culture hero, the "great *net*" (Strong 1929:100). In a tale recorded by Patencio, the Murray Hills are called *Wawashcaleit* (269), meaning "stripes on the hills. . .and the same stripes or streaks are there today." The name was given them by the Cahuilla culture hero *Evonganet* (Patencio 1943:53).

Murray Canyon was called *eit* (48), meaning "thief," by the "great *net*" (Strong 1929:100).

The area was rich in food resources. Throughout the spring and early summer water flows freely down this canyon. It is therefore rich in flora and fauna. Deer were commonly found near camps and mountain sheep at higher levels. Significant flora include palm trees, pinyon trees, yucca, many species of edible cacti, and other low shrubs common to the arid lands of southern California. These plants attract rodents and other animals which were used by the Cahuilla (Bean and Saubel 1972). See Bean and Vane (1983).

Martinez Canyon (117)

Martinez Canyon was, prior to European contact, the home of the *Wantcinakiktum* lineage of the Wildcat moiety. The *Īsilsiveyyaiutcem* also occupied the area, but at another and later period of time. The *Wantcinakiktum* originally came from *Ataki* (12) (Hidden Spring in the lower portion of Rockhouse Canyon) (Strong 1929:41; Bean field notes ca. 1960). The name "*wantcinakiktum*" also refers to a mountain in the Santa Rosas. Its exact location is not known.

The *Wantcinakiktum* lived at the village of *Pūichekiva* (182). When this village "broke up," they moved to Martinez Canyon and established a village called *Isilsiveyyaiutcem* (79). Strong felt that this village, whose exact location is unknown, was the original home of the clan before they moved to the desert. Contemporary descendants of the lineage include the present day Siva family, now for the most part associated with the Los Coyotes Reservation. Pablo Siva of the lineage was living at Martinez when Strong collected his data on the Cahuilla in the 1920s (1929:45).

When the *Wantcinakiktum* clan moved to the desert, they shared living space with the *Awilem* lineage, although they still had their own food gathering areas at Martinez Canyon where they went in the spring and early summer to gather cacti (1929:47). It was here that these families who had lived at the village *Puichekiva* (182) with the *Awilem* went when that village was abandoned (1929:47). Juan Siva recalled to Bean (ca. 1960) that the *Isilsiva* were at one time in the desert, and then moved into the mountains at the edge of Martinez, near Vallerie, and south of Rabbit Peak. The *Isilsiva* lived there, where there was a natural reservoir, and went back and forth to Borrego, planting watermelons, squash, corn, and beans. Juan Siva's grandfather said the rabbits were eating the plants so they built a cactus fence of *chukal* to keep rabbits out. The rabbit fence is still there in Collins Valley according to Katherine Siva Saubel. In the summer they were in the mountains harvesting pinyons. Afterward they went back to Borrego. After a while some of the men didn't like it, ill feelings of some kind developed, and so cloudbursts were sent to destroy the plantings. Rain washed the plants away so people couldn't plant any more. The *Isilsiva* then moved to *Wilyi* (279) in the Los Coyotes area. This was in the early 1800s.

The *Isilsivas* were *Wanchum* before they were *Isilsivas*. They originally lived in the Santa Rosa mountains and are closely related to the *Awilem*. They moved from the Martinez area because someone was killing their children (Bean ca. 1960).

Martinez Canyon was described by George Wharton James (1918:239-240). He recalls that the canyon contained ocotilla, *Yucca whipplei*, *Opuntia* and *Echinocacti*. He describes an elevated mesa

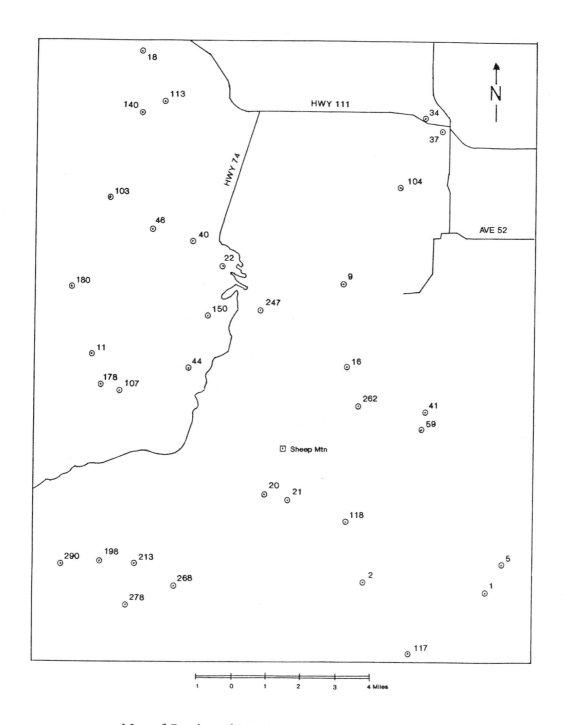

Map of Portion of Martinez and Toro Canyon Areas
Based on
Palm Desert, California 1959 Quadrangle, 15-minute Series, USGS Topographic Map

from which there is a spectacular view of the desert.

James says that Captain Pancho Lomas told him that the people of Torres came into the desert over the San Jacinto mountains, although originally, "in the beginning," they came from the east. They travelled for a long time on their trip over the San Jacintos. They were naked and had little food, and had to subsist on what plants and animals they could find. When they came to Martinez, they found that people had dug wells, so that mesquite trees and other food plants grew in abundance. Game was plentiful in the nearby mountains. It was an attractive spot, so they settled down in contentment.

After they lived there for a while, the waters rose in the Salton basin and drove them out of Martinez. They moved up Martinez Canyon, and finally to the village of Santa Rosa. The inland sea provided fish, which they caught with their stone fish traps, "rudely circular in shape. . .from two and one-half to nine feet in diameter, and give the impression they were built at low tide, so that as the water came in fish would enter and be caught" (James 1918:239-240). Wilke (1976) has demonstrated that the fish traps were built as the inland lake fell, causing fish to be plentiful on the shoreline. As the lake became too saline, the fish died.

James' informant also told him about the return to the desert when the water came down. "When the water first went down, the land had very little on it, only a few grasses, and the people did not have much to eat. Then the grasses grew more plentifully and soon the prickly pear and mesquite came and then all was well" (1918:239-240).

Numerous archaeological sites attest the long and intense human occupation of Martinez Canyon.

The Martinez Historical District (Martinez Indian Agency) is on the National Register of Historic Places.

Toro Canyon Area (121)

The *Toro* Canyon area was a major occupation area for the Cahuilla people in historic and prehistoric times. Today it is an area about which Cahuillas are concerned for cultural and historical reasons. The area contains a major late 19th century village site, *Mauulmii* (121) (Place of the Palm Tree), evidence of deep water wells, an historic cemetery, various hunting and gathering areas, and the like. Up above *Toro* are the fish traps (56) built along the shores of Lake Cahuilla and associated archaeological sites, including several village sites.

It is said to have been the home of the *Sawalakiktum* Cahuilla (Gifford 1918). Many other Cahuilla have used the canyon area in the past several generations. Most elderly or knowledgeable Cahuillas recall its use. The anthropological informants who have recalled it include Salvador Lopez, Juan Siva, Calistro Tortes, Alice Lopez, and Ruby Modesto. Gifford (1918), Merriam (field notes, date unknown), and Strong (1929:52) agree that the *Wakaikiktum* clan lived here. Gifford says that this clan originally lived near Warner's ranch, but was not Cupeño. Their location was probably in the Los Coyotes Canyon area (1918:190). Strong says the *Wakaikiktum* originally lived at *Tciuk* (226) "back in the Santa Rosa Mountains, then at *panuksi* (161) at the head of a canyon about seven miles south of Indio, and later came to *mauulmii*" (121) (1929:52). According to Strong, the *Wakaikiktum* (night heron) and the *Pañakauissiktum* (water fox) clans lived at *Mauulmii* in about the 1870s. The former occupied ten houses, three of them communal, and the latter, six houses. They shared the well (actually there were at least 3 wells here), which was probably dug by the *Pañakauissiktum* as earliest residents. There were two ceremonial houses, and each clan had its own area where plants were cultivated, and its own gathering area, presumably throughout the canyon.

Apparently the *Sewahilem* (mesquite that is not sweet) lineage also moved to *Mauulmii* from near La Mesa about 1895 (1929:52). Gifford also says the *Tamolañitcem* lineage, Wildcat moiety, lived at *Toro* (1918:190). There are frequent references in the literature to *Toro* Village, but it is not clear whether this is always in reference to the village known to Cahuillas as *Mauulmii* or there may at times be confusion with *Torres*, the location of the *Torres* Indian Reservation.

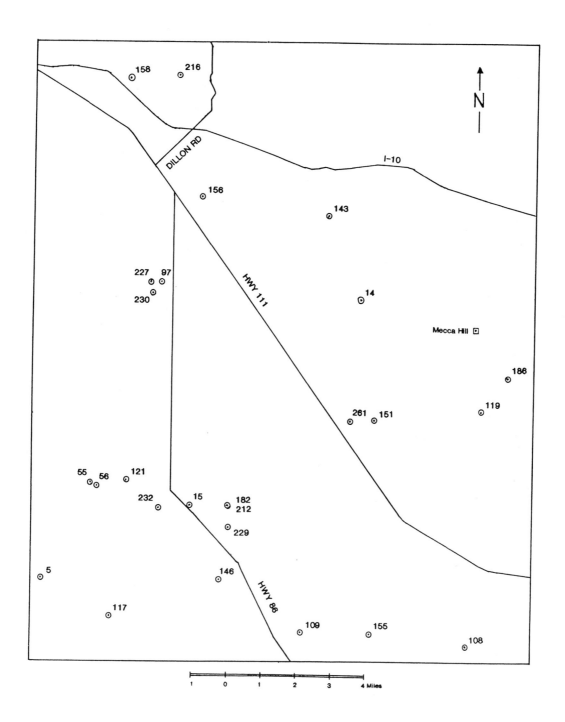

Portion of Toro and Martinez Areas
Based on the
Coachella, California, 1956, 15-minute Series, USGS Topographic Map

In one reference to *Toro* (121), Patencio tells of chiefs' calling a meeting in order to punish bad people. They are said to have gathered the warriors from *Toro* and *Morongo*, men from all tribes everywhere, and proceeded to *Yucaipa* to punish the malefactors--an indication that precontact Cahuilla Indians organized clans who lived some distance apart to go on the offensive (Patencio 1971).

With reference to a later period, Patencio says that the Pony Express ran through the desert via Palm Springs carrying the mail once a week between Yuma and San Bernardino, whence it was sent on to Los Angeles and San Francisco. The riders followed Indian trails, stopped where the Indians lived, and were supplied with food and water by the Indians, a fact confirmed by not only historical records, but also by Cahuilla oral tradition. One of the stops was El *Toro*, on the way from Martinez to Indian Wells. This was the same route taken by the Butterfield Trail, and later a country road (Johnston 1977).

Johnston says that the *Toro* area was heavily populated by Cahuillas in the 1850s and 1860s. "Cabezon lived here and more or less controlled his people from this point" (1977:120). There was a stop here for the Banning stage from an early period (1977:120).

The water supply at *Toro* came from wells dug by the Cahuilla. Several observers have commented on them.

> The whole valley of the Cabeson (Coachella Valley) is dotted with wells, most of them marking sites of homes long ago abandoned, the wells themselves being now only pits partly filled with sand, but many dug in the old way still remain, supporting life, and giving refreshment miles and miles away from the rocky walls where the streams of the mountains disappear in the sands. These wells are usually great pits of terraced sides leading down to the narrow holes at the bottom where water sparkles, built in such a way that a woman with an olla on her head can walk to the water's edge and dip her painted vessel full. . . .There is no question but that the Cahuilla learned of themselves to dig these wells, and this practice cannot be paralleled elsewhere among the American Indians [Barrows 1900:26-27].

Baldwin says that there were then eight Indian wells on the *Toro* Reservation lying in a straight line about half a mile (.8 km) long. From them, trenches four to eight feet (1.2 to 2.4 m) deep ran downward to clumps of mesquite trees which the wells irrigated. Not all the trenches, which ranged upward from 125 feet (38 m) in length, were still intact. The wells in 1938 were no longer in use and did not contain water, but mesquite trees and other vegetation marked their location (Baldwin 1938). A great many artifacts and features have been found at the site of *Mauulmii*, including round and rectangular house pits, tools of bone, stone, wood, and pottery. Some of the bone artifacts are incised. There are pipe fragments, bone awls, projectile points, scrapers and an enormous quantity of pottery. The floor of a ceremonial house was evident when Bean visited the site in 1960, as well as other house floors. A number of cremations were found at the site.

In the historical period people were buried in a cemetery. Despite the fact that it has been used in recent years, and in fact is still used, it has suffered a great deal of damage from marauders, pot hunters, and people who use the desert for recreation.

Overlooking *Toro* are some of the fish traps which the Cahuilla used, several hundred years ago, to catch fish at the shores of Lake Cahuilla (Wilke 1976:178-180).

Near the fish traps are petroglyphs which are also very significant for Cahuilla people. These are discussed in Chapter III.

There are numerous archaeological sites at the mouth of *Toro* Canyon and to its left and right. The sites are especially common along the ancient shoreline of Lake Cahuilla.

The three rows of fish traps along the shoreline are on the National Register of Historic Places.

The Santa Rosa and Rockhouse Canyon Areas

The area of Santa Rosa Indian Reservation, Nicholias (Nicolas) Canyon, and Rockhouse

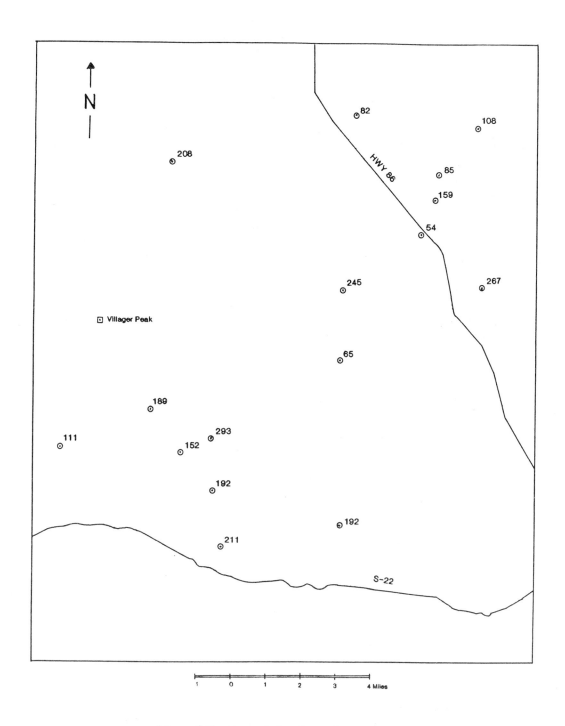

Map of Portion of the Santa Rosa Region
Based on
Rabbit Peak, California 1960, 15-minute Series USGS Topographic Map

Canyon on the southwestern slopes of the Santa Rosa Mountains is not only of considerable cultural and historic importance to scholars, but also has special significance to contemporary Cahuilla. Unfortunately for Native Americans and scholars, the area has been exploited by relic collectors for many years, and many private and public collections contain items collected in this area. Even so, the area is sufficiently intact that significant data could be expected from a carefully conducted ethno-archaeological study.

Rockhouse Canyon (194) has a central place in Cahuilla oral history. According to accounts provided by Captain Poncho Lomas in the second decade of this century, the Cahuilla long ago came from the east to an area west of the San Jacinto Mountains. Later they moved across the San Jacinto into the desert area at Martinez, northwest of the present Salton Sea. This area, where the water table was relatively high, provided abundant subsistence resources. When Lake Cahuilla rose in the Salton Basin the Cahuilla ascended Martinez Canyon (117), and settled down in the village of Santa Rosa (102), where they developed a rich lacustrine economy. When the waters fell, the Cahuilla returned to the valley (G. W. James 1918:239-240). This general account has been reported to us by other Cahuilla. Strong says that there were roughly two groups of Cahuilla in the southern Santa Rosa mountain areas in late aboriginal times, one group centered in Coyote Canyon (193) and one in the Santa Rosa Canyon (102) area. The latter area included both Old and New Santa Rosa (102) (206) and the village of *Natcuta* (130) in Horse Canyon (1929:144-147). ". . . at Old Santa Rosa, which is situated in a fork of Rock House Canyon, were two villages, *Kolwovakut* (102) and *Kewel* (101), and at 'new' Santa Rosa was the village of *Sewiu* (206). Several miles to the northwest was the old town of *Natcuta* (130), about one-half mile east of Horse Canyon" (1929:146).

The clan home of the *Costakiktum* was at *Sēwiā* (206) just south of Santa Rosa Mountain. In 1846 the *Costakiktum*, under the leadership of Juan Antonio, moved to Jurupa near Riverside and then to the San Timoteo Canyon (Strong 1929: 145-151). *Sēwiā* is perhaps the site Reed is referring to when he says a branch of the trail from Nicolas Canyon (133) to Santa Rosa Reservation leads to a village site where there used to be several Indian ollas until collectors found them and stole them (1963:126). Alice Lopez remembers going with her husband, Salvador Lopez, to the village of *Sēwiā*. She says there was still an old house there, and apple and pear trees (Vane field notes 1979).

Immediately to the west of the *Costakikaum* were the *Natcūtakiktum* at *Natcūta* (130) in Horse Canyon. Members of this clan also left the area under the leadership of Juan Antonio. Tomas Arenas was *net* of this clan in about 1850, one of four *nets* among the northern Cahuilla clans remembered at that time. In the 1860s four families of this clan, members of the Arenas family, lived at *Sēūpa* (204) on the Cahuilla reservation. In the 1920s two families, descended from one of these, were still extant (Strong 1929 :145-157). Five lineages of the *Wiwaīistam* clan lived in the Coyote Canyon area. One of these, the *Sauicpakiktum*, lived in Thousand Palm Canyon, off Collins Valley. After Juan Antonio led his group out of the Santa Rosa area, the *Sauicpakiktum* segmented and the two resulting lineages occupied *Sēwiā* (206), "New" Santa Rosa, and *Kewel* (101), in Rockhouse Canyon (Strong 1929:145, 148, 151, 158). "New" Santa Rosa village is sometimes called *We-wut-now-hu* (Barrows 1900:37; Kroeber 1925:694), raising the question of whether *We-wut-now-hu* and *Sēwiā* are the same village, or whether they are two villages each called "New Santa Rosa," a question that only a careful ethnoarchaeological study will resolve. Barrows noted, "Returning to the mountains once more, among the rocks and pines on the south side of the isolated summit of Torres is a rough little valley, traversed by a small, rapid stream, to which the Indians long ago penetrated. Here is the interesting village of Santa Rosa, *We-wut-now-hu* (206) (pines). These Indians make their homes during the winter months in the Coyote Canyon (193), a wide, sandy arm of the desert, thrust in south of Torres. Across this valley is the Coyote range of mountains. Up the sides of these mountains the Coahuillas found their way and established themselves in a beautiful and remote little glade, now known as San Ignacio (*Pa-cha-wal*) (166)" (Barrows 1900:34).

Early in the century George Wharton James reported, "We are aiming for the Indian village of Santa Rosa, perched high on the mountain of the same name" (1918:442). That would be presently the Santa Rosa Reservation. It was the Vandeventer Ranch. "Mr. Vandeventer tells us of the days when the Indians lived by the hundreds in the nearby valleys. But as civilization has crept closer to them they have mostly disappeared, smallpox and consumption having aided the vices of the white man in furthering their annihilation" (G. W. James 1918:443).

28

According to Al Benson, a prospector born at Fort Yuma in 1868 and interviewed by Smith (1942:112), the Cahuilla said that they were "driven into Rock House Canyon (194) by Indian wars." It is difficult to interpret information of this kind. The Cahuillas to whom Benson referred may have been talking about a pre-European conflict (Romero 1954) that drove their predecessors into the valley, or about the conflicts of the 1850s in the midst of which they themselves had moved to the canyon. These included the Garra revolt in which a confederation of Yuman-speakers from the Colorado River area and other southern California Indians under the leadership of Antonio Garra united against the vastly outnumbered Euroamericans in 1850s, and were vanquished only by the combined military forces of the United States and Cahuillas led by *Costakik* leader Juan Antonio. The leaders, including Antonio Garra, were caught in Los Coyotes Canyon and subsequently executed (Strong 1929:185,250; Phillips 1975).

In Rockhouse Valley the Cahuilla built their houses of rock piled up to about three feet (1 m) and roofed with juniper branches and brush. Some were round, and some, possibly built after contact with Mexicans, were square. Apparently priests from San Ignacio "Mission" at San Ignacio Rancho had a subsidiary mission in the canyon, coming there about once a month. The mission was built in the same style as the houses. Prospector Al Benson told Desmond Smith he remembered attending services there with his father when he was seven years old--about 1875 (Smith 1942:112-113).

Benson described the place where the Cahuilla cremated the dead. Two large slabs of rock were set on edge on either side of a pit in which a fire was built. There was a drawing of a man with outstretched arms on one rock. The ashes and remains were placed in ollas which were buried in the cemetery below the mission building. Benson said there remained none of these which had not been broken by land movement in the vicinity. Smith had heard an unconfirmed rumor that someone had taken thirty crematory ollas from side canyons in the area (Smith 1942:112-113). The use of crematory ollas is not otherwise reported for the Cahuillas, but is reported for their neighbors, the *Kumeyaay*.

There was a severe smallpox epidemic about 1875. Afterward there was a great deal of moving, as people fled homes where relatives had died. It may have been at this time that some *Sauicpakiktum* people left Rockhouse Valley for the Torres-Martinez area, e.g., the *Wantciñakik-tamianawitcem* who went to *Tūva* (265) (Strong 1929:41), and that other people came to take their place. So many people died that whole lineages and clans became extinct or nearly extinct. Our recent search of mission records suggests that over half of the Cahuilla lineages known in 1820 were no longer remarked by the time ethnographic work among the Cahuilla began about 1900. Apparently some marriages that violated traditional rules took place at this time, and occasionally two or more clans consolidated to make one ceremonial unit. In at least one instance a ceremonial leader sent his ceremonial shell money to the *net* of another clan, and buried the ceremonial bundle of his clan after a last mourning ceremony, a formal recognition that a lineage or clan was no longer extant (Strong 1929:152-163).

In the late 19th century local white pioneers stayed away from Rockhouse Valley, knowing they were not welcome there. One outsider who ignored advice not to go into the area had his horse killed and sustained a bullet wound in his leg. In 1906 a local prospector found two horses tied up in the valley without food or water. He let them loose, but told two friends who were going prospecting about them. They entered Rockhouse Valley from Hidden Spring up Rockhouse Canyon and camped near a lone cottonwood tree near water. Looking around, they found one dead horse and clothing and camping equipment. A blanket had blood on it and two utensils had bullet holes in them. The next day, while panning for gold, one of them "looked up on the side of the hill, and there stood an old Indian with a 30-30 rifle on his shoulder and carrying a forked stick in the other hand. . . . After talking with the old fellow for awhile, they invited him to their camp and asked him to eat with them. The Indian accepted the invitation, but would not take any of the food until he had seen them eat some of it." He told them there was gold in abundance to the south, apparently in an effort to discourage them from staying in the valley. Making inquiries subsequently in the Coachella Valley, they learned at Mecca "that two men had walked out of Rockhouse saying their horses had been poisoned, and had then taken a train for Imperial Valley" (Reed 1963:72-74; 127). There are other accounts of Cahuillas protecting their area at this late date.

In 1909, Wayland Smith, in a Sequoyah League publication, reported, "The Santa Rosa Indians have asked for and are to receive their old home at Van De Venter Flat, called by them *Se'-o-ya*, pleasant view. Land has been reserved for them here, and water sufficient for present needs appropriated" (Smith 1909).

Rockhouse Valley (194) contains the ruins of several villages, spectacular as California archaeological sites go because they contain the ruins of the rockwalled houses. One of them is known as "Old Santa Rosa" (U.S. War Department, U.S. Army, Corps of Engineers 1944). It is not possible to say whether this is *Kewil* (101) without further investigation. It is well served by trails.

The Tortes and Andreas families were the last members of the *Sauicpakiktum* to live in Rockhouse Valley. Reed says that "portions of the rock walls of the Tortes home are still to be seen in the southern portion of Rockhouse Valley where there are the remains of three other rockhouses-- one of them the home of the Andreas family." Reed goes on to say that half a mile east of the Tortes rockhouse was a watering place near a cottonwood tree from which the Tortes and Andreas families probably obtained their water--perhaps Cottonwood "spring" (Reed says it was not really a spring, but a place where the water was close to the surface). "At the base of *Toro* peak, in the northern portion of Rockhouse Valley, near a little spring of water are the remains of another rockhouse Indian village. . . . To the south of the little spring is a rock circle that is still very much intact, and even though this wall is circular instead of being made with four corners as the others were, it no doubt was one of their dwelling places." Reed also describes the ruins of another rectangular dwelling place and says that there are other places without rock walls that appear to have been house sites (Reed 1963:122-123).

Calistro Tortes was the last Cahuilla to live in Rockhouse Valley. He was the son of Manuel Tortes, "chief of the Rockhouse Valley Indians" (Reed 1963:122), and brother of Celestin Tortes, who was David Prescott Barrows' principal guide on his research trips in the Cahuilla area. Calistro was born sometime between 1860 and 1880 and lived into the 1960s. According to Bean's field notes, he was the last of the Cahuillas living then who had lived at Old Santa Rosa (102). Reed says that he was born at Hidden Springs (1963:120), in the village of *Ataki* (12). Juan Siva also identified the Hidden Spring village as *Ataki* (Bean field notes, ca. 1960). Strong says that this was the place from which the three desert Cahuilla clans, the *Watciñakiktum*, *Palpunivikiktum*, and *Watcinakik-tamianawitcem* clans originally came. The first two of these later lived at *Puichekiva* (182) near Martinez, and the third at *Tuva* (265) (Strong 1929:41). The residents of Rockhouse Valley are said to have come down to the Hidden Spring (12) area in winter to take advantage of its warmer climate and winter vegetation and hunting opportunities (Bean field notes, ca. 1960). *Ataki* was on a mesa above a hidden spring. It is probable that there were both early and late occupations here. Some house pits were distinguishable in the 1930s. An amateur archaeologist from El Cajon dug out burials here in the 1930s. All had Caucasian material in them. One skull had a bandana handkerchief about the head (Anonymous, ca. 1938).

Merriam's notes contain several references to the Santa Rosa/Rockhouse Valley people. According to him, the *Pow'-we-yam* clan occupied the west slope of the San Jacinto Mountains south of Latitude 33 40'. These were the western neighbors of the *Sow'-wah-pah-keek-tem* people who were the "Santa Rosa Mountain tribe." To the north were the *Wah'-ki-chi'-m-kut-tem* (or *Sow-wis-pan-kik-tem* or *Sauispakiktum*) at Vandeventer Flat at a later date. He gives the village there the Cahuilla name *Sa-we-ah* or *Seu-yah*. He says the original name was *Sowis-is-pakh*. Such naming is typical in Cahuilla (Field notes: X/2300-11/G57). *Sauispakiktum* is the lineage name of the Tortes family. In Cahuilla the word *Sawish* refers to a flat breadcake made from acorn meal and water. The family subsequently took the name Tortes, from the Spanish "tortilla," for their family name.

Strong did not locate "new" Santa Rosa at Vandeventer Flat (1929:145), and it would appear that the village there may have been named *Sa-we-ah* after the *Sauispakiktum* moved "back" there in 1909 (Smith 1909).

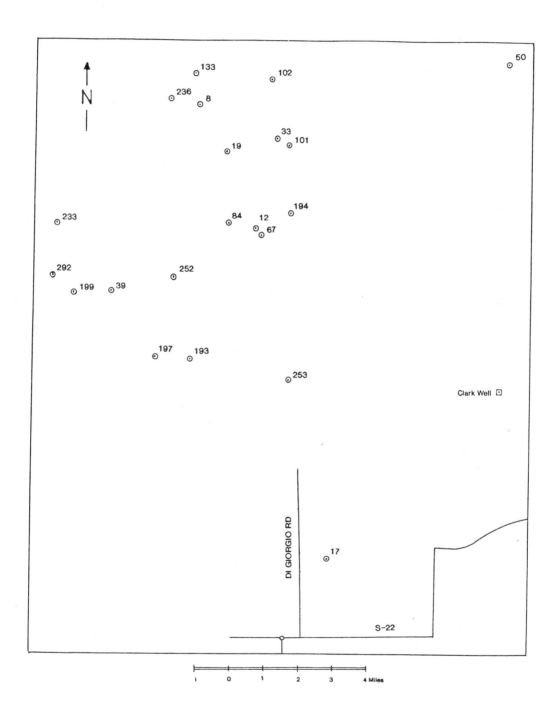

Map of Portion of Santa Rosa Region and Los Coyotes Region
Based on the
Clark Lake, California 1960 Quadrangle, 15-minute Series, USGS Topographic Map

31

Rockhouse Canyon is mentioned frequently in Cahuilla oral literature. In a migration myth recounted to Hansjacob Seiler by Joe Lomas in 1964, ancestors of the Cahuilla at Torres, led by the hero Yellow Body, traveled from Rockhouse Canyon to where the Torres Reservation is now located, and from there to Cupa Hot Springs (Warner Hot Springs), where they entered the water, to live on as immortal brown dogs (Seiler 1970:64-73). Patencio says that Yellow Body settled for a time at Deep Canyon (247). At the same time another culture hero named *Mul li kik* settled at Vandeventer Flat, which was called *San we yet* (206). Yellow Body sent his dog to the people at *San we yet* to choose a family for Yellow Body's sister to marry into. The dog passed by the houses of those who tried to entice him to come to them, and went to the last house, where they fed him. The dog having reported favorably on the householders, Yellow Body sent his sister to marry into that family (Patencio 1943:37-38).

The trail between Santa Rosa Reservation and Rock House Valley leads through Nicholias (sometimes spelled "Nicolas") (133) Canyon. This trail passes Nicolas Spring, the source of the stream which has cut the canyon. "On the ridge to the south and east of the spring, are the remains of the old Nicolas rockhouse, and in a basin to the north and east of the site is a row of cotton wood trees that were no doubt planted by the Indians. Along the side of the hill below the spring is evidence of a ditch through which the Indians probably ran water from the spring to water their garden" (Reed 1963:122-125).

Nicolas Spring and Canyon were named after Nicolas Guanche, the last of the Guanche family to live there. He died an old man between 1914 and 1921. Members of the Guanche family still live at Santa Rosa Reservation. There are metates and weathered pictographs on the boulders to the west of the stream, suggesting that the canyon has been used for hundreds of years.

The peak of Santa Rosa Mountain (278) is considered sacred by the Cahuilla. It is typical of the Cahuilla cosmological tradition, as of many other traditions, to consider such places sacred. It is associated with seeing "high" and distant and remote places as the homes of sacred beings or the places where they touch down when they visit "middle earth." This peak, like *Tahquitz* Peak, also in Cahuilla territory, is such a place. Sacred persons, such as Cahuilla *net'em* (lineage or clan administrators) or *puvulum* (shamans) frequently visited such places to receive inspiration or power. The Cahuilla, according to Patencio, called the Santa Rosa mountain *Weal um mo* (278). The culture hero Yellow Body rested there to remove a troublesome cholla cactus thorn from his foot. He threw a thorn on top of a large rock, where it grew, and named the mountain *Weal um mo* (Patencio 1943:38). Bean's field notes (ca. 1960) indicate that the mountain was called *Sen villet*. Barrows recorded the name *Cawish wa-wat-acha*, or the "mighty mountain" (Barrows 1893-1900).

A ridge of the mountain was reportedly named *Hiawat* (65) (Chase 1919).

There is at least one petroglyph site, located at the upper end of the east fork of Rockhouse Canyon. The petroglyphs are on the face of a large granite boulder. A few sherds were found at the site. Steward (1929:95) and others have described it.

Meighan surveyed sites in Rockhouse Canyon, Collins Valley, Indian Canyon, Coyote Creek, and Clark Dry Lake in the late 1950s (1959). One hundred seventy-three sites were discovered which dated to about A.D. 1000. He pointed out that an enormous amount of looting of archaeological material had taken place, perhaps the most anywhere in California. Sites even in the most remote and inaccessible parts of the Borrego Park suffered from the collecting and digging of vandals. Most sites consist mostly of surface remains. In some, these had been picked over intensively and only a few small potsherds were found which would warrant further investigation or excavation. Active digging was going on by relic collectors during the time of his survey. Other archaeologists since that time have noted that continuing vandalism and damage from recreational vehicles are significant destroyers of archaeological or historic evidence in this area.

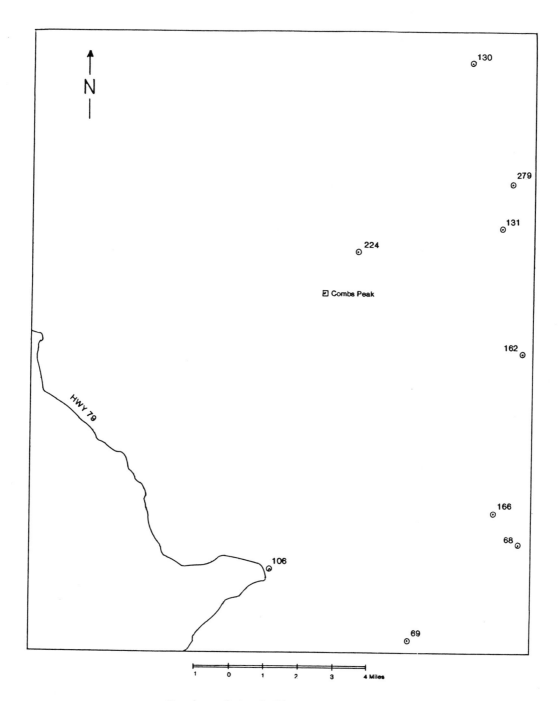

Portion of the Collins Valley Region
Based on the
Warner Springs, California 1961 Quadrangle, 15-minute USGS Topographic Map

VI. INDEX TO PLACE NAME VARIATIONS

Indian Spring (76)
Indian Wells (Deep Well)   Cov in ish (34)
Indian Wells Point   Cow on vah al ham ah (37)
Indio Hills, South Ridge   Akawene (7)
Indio Mountain or Coyote Mountain   Alhauik (9)
Invitca   Eng be cha (49)
Ish el wat tow ta um ali (78)
Isil Kaw-we-vah-ah (77)
Ísilsíveyaiutcem (79)
Íva (80)
Ívawakik (81)
Íviatim (82)
I was wa ba all (83)
Jackass Flat (84)
Juan Razon's Allotment (85)
Kakwawit (86)
Kalahal (87)
Kauissimtcem hemkí (89)
Kauistanalmū (90)
Kaukwicheki (91)
Kaunukvela   Cow nuk kal kik tem (36)
Ka-vi-nish   Cov in ish (34)
Kawis Ah-mov-vash (92)
Kawishmu (94)
Kawish-wa-wat-acha (93)
Kawis-pa-miya (95)
Kekliva (96)
Kelewutkwíikwinut   (Ekwawinet) (97)
Kéwil   Kiwil (101)
Key wat wah he wen e (98)
Kick ke san lem mo (99)
Kish chowl (100)
Kistacavel (Kish chowl) (100)
Kiwil (101)
Kolwovakut (102)
Konkistū-uinut (103)
Ko-pa   Kūpa (106)
Kōtevewit (104)
Kow wish so kalet (105)
Kūpa (Ko-pa) (106)
Kwa-le-ki (107)
La Mesa   Temal-wa-hish (230)
Lake Cahuilla, Ancient Salton Sea (108)
La-wil-van (Sivel) (109)
Leaning Rock   Waívas (270)
Lincoln Peak (110)
Little Clark Lake (111)
Little Paradise Spring ?   Paskwa (165)
Long Valley   Hunwit hekik (74)
Mad Woman Spring (112)
Magnesia Spring (113)
Magnesia Springs Canyon   Pah-wah'-te (140)
Mala (114)
Malal (115)
Mal-ki (116)
Martinez Canyon (117)
Martinez Mountain ?   Wantciña

(118)
Maswut helaanut (119)
Mauit (120)
Mauūlmií (121)
Me ahs cal et   Míaskalet (122)
Mecca Hills   Quawish-Ulish (186)
Mecca Hills Village   Kawis-pa-miya (95)
Metate point, North Point, Chino Canyon   Malal (115)
Míaskalet (Me ahs cal et) (122)
Millyillilikalet (123)
Mission Creek Area   Yamisevul (124)
Mission Creek home of Kilyiñakiktum clan (287)
Mission Creek Trail (288)
Moreno Valley (289)
Morongo Reservation   Mal-ki (116)
Mountain Home Spring (290)
Mowal (292)
Mow it check mow win it (291)
Mud Volcanoes, Salton Sea   Par-powl (163)
Mukunpat (124)
Mum yum muck ca (125)
Murray Canyon   Éit (48)
Murray Hill   Sēwitckul (207)
Murray Hills   Wa wash ca le it (269)
Murray Hills Trail (126)
Na che wit (127)
Na hal log wen et (128)
Naíalwawaka (129)
Natcūta (130)
Nauhañavitcem Village (131)
New Santa Rosa   We-wut now hu (206)
Ng natches pie ah (132)
Nicholias (Nicolas) Canyon, Spring, and Village (133)
Ninkicmu (134)
Num na sh b al (135)
"Old Guadalupe Trail"   Tukut (262)
Old Santa Rosa   Kiwil (101)
Old Santa Rosa Village   Kolwovakut (102)
One Horse Point   E va we (52)
One Palmn Creek (136)
Ow kee ve lem (137)
Pa cale (138)
Pa hal ke on a (139)
Pah-wah'-te (140)
Paint Island (141)
Paklic (142)
Palaíyil (143)
Palhanikalet   (Tahquitz Falls) (144)
Palhilikwintu (145)
Pal híliwit (146)
Paliliem hemkí (147)
Palkausinakela   Paltūkwic kaíkaíawit (159)
Palm Bowl   Panoquk (163)

Palm Canyon, Entrance To Tekelkukuaka (228)
Palm Canyon Trail (148)
Palm Canyon Trail Shrines (149)
Palm Canyon Village   Tatmílmí (165)
Palm Canyon Wash (?)   Kick ke san lem mo (99)
Palm Canyon Wash, Unnamed point   Cow wis to lek ets (38)
Palm Springs, Agua Caliente   Sec he (203)
Palm Springs Station   Haviñavitcum Territory (63)
Palms to Pines Trail (150)
Palmulūkalet (151)
Palo Verde Canyon (152)
Palpísa (153)
Pal pis o wit (154)
Palpūniviktum hemkí (155)
Palseta   Palsētahut (156)
Palsētahut (156)
Palsētamul (Pal-so'nul) (157)
Pal tē-wat (158)
Paltūkwic kaíkaíawit (Palkausinakela) (159)
Paluknavitcem   (Stubbe Canyon and Village) (160)
Pa-nach-sa (Panūksí) (161)
Panūksí   Pa-nach-sa (161)
Panoquk (Palm Bowl) (162)
Panyik (Andreas Canyon Village) (10)
Par-powl   ("Mud Volcanoes", Salton Sea) (163)
Pasíawha (164)
Paskwa (Agua Bonita or Little Paradise Spring) (3)
Pat-cha-wal (San Ignacio) (166)
Pa:tsh yara:'nka'Wanet (167)
Pauata (168)
Pauí (Cahuilla) (169)
Paukí (170)
Pa ute em (171)
Pelican Island (174)
Pe on bel (Píonvil) (172)
Pe ya hot mor am mah   (Song Point) (173)
Piatopa   Pisata (176)
Pierce Ranch and Springs (175)
Pínalata (177)
Pinyon Flat (178)
Píonvil   Pe on bel (172)
Pisata (Piatopa) (176)
Place West of Toro (179)
Point Happy   Cow on vah al ham ah (37)
Poo on loo la   Pul lo cla (183)
Poo ool   Pow ool (181)
Potrero Spring (180)
Pow ool   (Poo ool, Hidden Lake) (181)
Pūichekiva (182)
Pul lo cla (183)
Pūllūvil (Rock at Tachevah Falls) (184)

Warner Hot Springs (106)
Watcicpa (273)
Wavaai (274)
Wa wash ca le it (269)
Weal um mo ? Wilamū (278)
Weh-ghett (20,275)
West Fork, Palm Canyon Hunting
Trail (276)
We-wut now hu (206)
Whitewater River, Mouth of Wani
(272)
Wiasmul (277)
Wilamu (278)
Wildcat Mortar Rock Tukut kaw-
we-vah-ah (263)
Wiliya (279)
Windy Point, Whitewater Point
Tama (219)
Wiwaiistam Wiliya (279)
Woh hut cli a low win it (280)
Wonderstone Trail (293)
Yamisevul (124)
Yan heck e (281)
Yauahic (282)
You koo hul ya me (283)
Young ga vet wit ham pah va (285)
You ye va al (284)
Yum ich you (286)

VII. PLACES IN THE CAHUILLA LANDSCAPE
An Alphabetical Arrangement

Agua Alta Canyon (1)

This canyon branches off from Martinez Canyon. One fork begins on the flank of Martinez Mountain and the other drains the site of the Cahuilla village *Ahl-wah-hem'-ke* (Casa de Cuerva) from which the Cahuillas went to the Salton Sea (before it subsided) to fish and collect. It has stands of carrizo, useful as a building material.

Agua Alta Spring (2)

This spring is on the Cactus Spring Trail near Pinyon Alta Flat, and was an important source of water for those who used the trail. It goes through pinyon juniper woodland.

Agua Bonita Spring (3)

This spring was along the main trail up Palm Canyon, where it would have been an important source of water for travellers, hunters, and those going up the canyon for ceremonial purposes. It is possibly the site of *Tatmilmi* (q.v.).

Agua Fuerte Spring (4)

The name of this spring means "strong" water. It can be assumed to have supplied a substantial water supply for the upper West Fork of Palm Canyon. It lies on the trail between Hermit's Bench and Cedar Spring.

Ahl-wah-hem'-ke (5)   Casa de Cuerva
"House of many ravens"
   A place on Santa Rosa Mountain held in religious regard (Chase 1919:72). This large flat area lies above the village of *Toro*. It has been pointed out as the place where ritual activities, such as boys' initiation rites, occurred in "the old days."

Aiakaīc (6)   San Jacinto Peak

Named by great *net* (Strong 1929:100-101).

Akawene (7)   Indio Hills, South Ridge

"Place name for the long ridge in the mountains east of Indio," possibly the ridge in the Indio Hills extending southeast of Indio Mountain. Behind the ridge stand the Little San Bernardino Mountains, another possibility. The *Akawenekiktum* clan who lived at *Palsētahut* ("salt water") near Coachella took their name from *Akawene (Stro*ng 1929:42).

Alder Canyon (8)

With Nicholias Canyon to the north, Alder Canyon formed the western part of Rockhouse Valley.

Alhauik (9)   Indio Mountain or Coyote Mountain
"No opening"

A mountain that the "great *net*" described as a "hill south of Indio," at southeastern boundary of *Kauisik* territory (Strong 1929:101). There are large trail shrines along an aboriginal trail on this mountain that may mark the boundary.

Andreas Canyon Village (10)   *Panyik*

The *Paniktum* lineage of the Palm Springs Cahuilla occupied Andreas Canyon. The version of the migration story told by Francisco Patencio has it that the second son of *Ca wis ke on ca* left Palm Springs and moved first to Little Tacheva and then among the rock pile at Tahquitz, *Cock wo wit*, and finally moved to a place near the mouth of Palm Canyon. "His older brother gave him the name *Pi ye now it e esa*, ... Then he gave him the line of his section of land. He gave him land from what is now Idyllwild down to Palm Canyon, through the west side of the Murray Hills; then across the Little Canyon of One Palm near the beginning of Andreas Club Road, north on Andreas Canyon" (Patencio 1943:90).

According to Strong, the "great *net*" very long ago brought his people first to *Watcicpa* (Redland junction), then to *Īva*, a hot spring north of *Soboba*, to *Kekliva*, a mountain north of *Soboba*, and then to *Panyik* at the mouth of San Andreas Canyon (1929:100). This place name is associated with the lower San Andreas and Palm Canyons.

Patencio says that there used to be painted signs, pictographs, all over the country, marking trails and conveying other important information. Only some of them are still understood. They have been replaced by printed signs and road markers. "People no longer depended on them for the way and water. There are the painted sign marks in Andreas Canyon, but no one reads them today, they are fast fading now" (Patencio 1943:103).

Members of the *Paniktum* lineage continue to live near here on Andreas ranch, and continue many of the traditions of the *Paniktum* Cahuilla. Anthony Andreas, Jr., the family head, serves as Tribal Historian for the Agua Caliente Indian Reservation.

Asbestos Spring (11)

This spring lay at the northwestern corner of Pinyon Flat at the end of the trail from Palm Canyon. It was an important source of water for people harvesting pinyon nuts at Pinyon Flat.

Ataki (12)

Hidden Springs Village
Rockhouse Canyon

According to Juan Siva (Bean 1960), Hidden Springs is the location of the Cahuilla village, *Ataki*, the original home of the *Wantcinakiktum* and *Palpunivikiktum* clans of the Wildcat moiety. The site is on a mesa above a hidden spring. It is possible that both early and late occupations are evidenced here. Some house pits were distinguishable in the 1930's. All had Caucasian material in them. One skull had a bandana handkerchief around the head" (Anonymous ca. 1938). A deeply worn trail leads from Coyote Canyon along the ridge above Box Canyon to Butler Canyon, then across Jackass Flat to Hidden Spring (Schad 1986:198-199). Another well-used trail connects the village of San Ignacio in the valley at the head of Borrego Palm Canyon with the village at Santa Catarina Spring in Coyote Canyon. "West of San Ignacio, this trail continued to the hot springs at what we now know as Warner Springs. East of Santa Catarina Spring, a branch of the trail continued through Box Canyon to another village at Hidden Spring" (Schad 1986:90).

Awelmū (13)

A large rock between *Pĩonvil* and *Tama* (q.v.) named after the first of the great *net's* three dogs (Strong 1929:101). It lay somewhere beyond where the second bridge on the highway from Palm Springs to Whitewater is located and Whitewater.

Andreas Canyon: Toll booth for tourist entering the Indian Canyons

From the 1920s on, the Indian Canyons were a popular tourist attraction in Palm Springs. They were also a source of revenue for the Agua Caliente Band. This picture was probably taken some time during the 1930s. Note the ramada, a traditional structure providing shade for the booth.

Awelpitcava (14)
"Dog lying by the trail"

A village east or southeast of Thermal, occupied by the *Wavitcem* lineage of the *Kauwicpauméauitcem* Cahuilla, Wildcat moiety (Strong 1929:41). This group was under the control of Cabezon in the nineteenth century. "Its main food gathering territory was in the eastern hills." All members were dead by the 1920s (Strong 1929:41, 54-55). Schwenn believes this village was located at the base of the Mecca Hills between the mouths of the Three Fingers Canyons at the east end of Airport Boulevard and Phantom Canyon, the next large canyon to the southeast of the Three Fingers.

Awilsīlhiwiniva (15)
"Where the willow tree is standing"

The home of the *Awilem* and *Wantciñakiktum* groups before they moved to Martinez, *Puichekiva* (Strong 1929:44,48).

The site of the village is about three-quarters of a mile west of the Martinez Indian Reservation tribal buildings.

Bear Creek Palm Oasis (16)

This is one of the many palm oases in the Cahuilla area (Henderson 1961:26). Even though there is no ethnographic data for the site, it can be assumed that it is a highly sensitive place to Native Americans because of the presence of a *Washingtonia filifera* eco-niche (Bean 1966; Bean and Saubel 1972:145-149).

Borrego Valley (17)

"They [Yellow Body, his mother, wife & dog] crossed the desert (Borrego Valley) and went to a hot spring which is now called Warner's Hot Spring" (Patencio 1943:39).

Bradley Canyon (18)

This canyon goes from the desert to a series of trails which connected many villages, approximately along the route of Highway 111. The canyon was a hunting and gathering area. Patencio (1943:71), for example, mentions hunting and gathering in this general area. He mentions specifically Magnesia Spring Canyon and Cathedral Canyon. Bradley Canyon is near the Murray Hills trail.

Buck Ridge (19)

Buck Ridge forms the southern boundary of Rockhouse Valley. Its rugged character has kept the valley isolated.

Cactus Springs Area (20)

The Cactus Springs area is one of the most sacred areas for the Cahuilla who lived in the desert, and one of the last ones untouched by modern developments. It contains the site of a village named *Tev-utt*, "The Place of the Pinyon Trees." The area is mapped as Little Pinyon Flat. The site of *Tev-utt* contains many bedrock mortar grinding places, smooth rock floors where people used to dance, and many pictographs and petroglyphs. Four important trails go from here to the west, northeast, southeast, and southwest. Some of them are worn two feet deep in places.

The area still contains many plants and animals which were traditionally used by the Cahuilla, including a pinyon tree that is thought to be the "largest one anywhere." This is considered a sacred tree. The area is one of the few places where certain traditional medicine plants can still be found.

Cactus Spring Trail (21)

This important trail runs from Pinyon Flat near the old settlement of Nightingale to Cactus Spring on Little Pinyon Flat in the Cactus Springs area, and continues to Pinyon Alta Flat on the southern slopes of Martinez Mountain, and thence to Martinez Canyon. Near Cactus Springs another trail branches off northeastward along Guadalupe Creek down to La Quinta and still another goes westward toward the Santa Rosa Mountain.

Katherine Saubel recalls that this was a trail by which her mother was taken as a young girl from the desert to the mountain home of her father's family when she was betrothed. It was also the trail used by people travelling to "*Nukil*" (funeral ceremonies) from some desert to some mountain villages.

Carrizo Creek (22)

A major trail, the Palms to Pines trail, ran along this creek from the Palm Desert area to Pinyon Flat.

Ca wish is mal (23)   Cathedral Canyon
"Painted rock"

A place in Cathedral Canyon was named *Ca Wish is mal* by the Cahuilla culture hero, *Evon ga net* (Patencio 1943:53). It is an important site for Cahuilla culture history.

Evon ga net, laying out land for different tribes of his people, went from Eagle Canyon and the springs that he named *E pah*, to Cathedral Canyon, which he called *Ca wish is mal* (Strong 1929:101).

The name may refer to deposits of a green ore in an old prospect on the east side of the canyon about the middle of Section 9.

Cedar Spring (24)

A spring west of Virgin Spring on the same trail. At Cedar Spring the trail branches, one branch going northeastward to Cactus Spring.

Chaparrosa Spring (25)

This spring, on the eastern slopes of Chaparrosa Peak and at the head of Chaparrosa Wash would have been a source of water for Pass Cahuilla and Serrano people who hunted and gathered in the Sawtooth Range.

Chee mo ke wen e (26)   Tahquitz Canyon
"A deep narrow canyon" (Patencio 1943:97)

"It was for this reason that the Palm Springs Indians were living in the cliffs at the north of Tahquitz Canyon when the Pony Express rider was killed. From this place they could see below.

They watched for strangers coming, and hid their children in the caves and cracks of the cliffs" (Patencio 1943:77; 1971:21, 22).

Chis hill mo (27)   Skunk Cabbage Meadow?
"Twins"

"Over on the top, where the Indian tobacco was gathered, he [*Ka wis ke on ca*] called that table top of pine trees *Chis hill mo* . . ." (Patencio 1943:96).

According to Schwenn, most of the area between Idyllwild and Mount San Jacinto and Hidden Lake is covered with pines which makes location of this place difficult. There is no information available as to the location of the Indian tobacco. However, one possible location for *Chis hill mo* is Skunk Cabbage Meadow, which is southwest of Hidden Lake, between the Lake and Tahquitz (Lily) Rock. The meadow is named for the skunk cabbage that grows there.

Chow o hut (28)   Little Tachiva (Tacheva)
"Wild plum"

The second son of culture hero *Ca wis ke on ca* "moved to the green spot back of Palm Springs to what is now known as Little Tachiva . . ." (Patencio 1943:90).

Little Tachiva is a canyon near Dry Falls (Tachevah Canyon) with a smaller rock monolith.

Clark Lake Dune Village (29)

This village site lies at the end of the trail from Rabbit Peak. It is about two acres in area, the largest in the region. The oldest occupation is on an old dune surface at the north end of the site. This had been exposed by erosion. At the east end of the area on top of late dunes and a gravelly wash at the base of the Santa Rosa Mountains are the remains of a village presumably occupied at a later date. It is near mesquite and agave gathering places and was probably a winter dwelling place. Ben Squier, a relic collector, found a cremation associated with glass points and scrap iron here, and Malcolm Rogers found two cremations which had been washed out. One was associated with small-mouthed water ollas of 'scoured' wear, two granite pestles, one granite mortar, two chalcedony points, and a granite mano. The other cremation was associated with a burnished pipe of 'rid' wear and an incised, small-mouthed, buff-ware canteen three inches high.

The Clark Lake petroglyph site lies at the base of the Santa Rosa Mountains, just east of the mouth of Rockhouse Canyon. The petroglyphs, which have been interpreted as being of an early Cahuilla type, are pecked into the reddish-brown patina of the boulders, which spread out for a hundred feet along the Clark Lake Petroglyph Trail, which leads from them to Old Santa Rosa (Anonymous ca. 1938). There are agave fiber rubs associated with the petroglyphs. These may be the same petroglyphs described and photographed by Reed (1963:116).

The Clark Lake Rock Feature near Clark Well, an important water source in the Colorado Desert, is near the southwest boundary of Rockhouse Canyon Cahuilla people's territory. This may be one of the most important Cahuilla sites in the Santa Rosa Mountains. It lay near the junction of trails, and there were pictographs and cobble shrines nearby. The feature consisted of boulders placed a foot and a half apart in a circle measuring 70 feet in diameter.

Cock wo wit (30)   Large Rock Pile
"Piled Boulders"   Tahquitz Canyon

The second son of culture hero *Ca wis ke on ca* "moved across Tahquitz among the large rock pile there . . .. There he lived for a long time" (Patencio 1943:90).

This was probably the rocky area on the stream terrace northeast of Tahquitz Canyon on the south side of the creek.

Con kish wi qual (31)

This place in Whitewater Wash was named *Con kish wi qual* by the Cahuilla culture hero, *Evon ga net*. The name means "two desert willows" (Patencio 1943:54). See discussion of the Whitewater area. It lay west of Indian Avenue and North of Chino Canyon.

Cottonwood Canyon (32)

This area between Stubbe and Whitewater Canyons was one of the many areas occupied by *Wanikik* Cahuilla. There are many Cahuilla sites in the canyon mouth, from which all artifacts have long since been removed.

Cottonwood Spring (33)

A spring in Rockhouse Valley. This is a site where water is close to the surface, but it is not a spring. It is half a mile from a village site, possibly that of *Kewel*. After rains, the water here attracts "coyotes, bobcats, foxes, a few wild burros, desert birds, and an occasional Big Horn Sheep" (Reed 1963:122; Bean field notes, ca. 1960).

Cov in ish (Ka-vi-nish) (34)   Indian Wells (Deep Well)
"Low or hollow place"

Merriam (field notes, date unknown) noted that the tribes who lived at Indian Wells ranged south into the desert mountains to Indio Mountain and Sheep Mountain and west to Deep Canyon.

Aswitseï's people settled here, where the water did not reach, until the water began to go back, according to the migration legend of the *Sēwahilem* clan, as told by Akasem Levi (Strong 1929:86).

Of the people who were led over San Gorgonio Pass by the five head men, those led by Sungrey settled at Indian Wells. One of the head men Sungrey, feeling that his time was about gone, became the first palm tree, to which all of the people came to eat the fruit (Patencio 1943:101).

Eagle Flower, seeing a palm tree at Indian Wells, "recognized the Palm tree as one of his own people. Then they talked to each other, and both began to cry together" (Patencio 1943:42).

Cow is ic el a (Kauisikī) (35)   Aunt Rock
"The fox's dress"

"In the old days of the First People, the Fox Tribe that is now known as the Palm Springs Indians were living at the mouth of Tahquitz Canyon among the cliffs. A young woman of much power surprised her people by turning into a large rock. This rock sits upon a big flat boulder at the side of Tahquitz Creek, on entering the canyon, or just across from the Echo Cliffs. The rock is square in shape, and has a white, pointed top. This rock was never there before the young woman disappeared.

"The young woman's name was *Cow is ic el a*, meaning the fox's dress. The Indians say that this rock often takes the form of a woman, from across the creek. She has always been honored among here tribe, who call the rock their aunt, and the rock is known among the Indians as the 'Aunt Rock'" (Patencio 1943:73).

". . . coming north along the eastern edge of the mountains bordering the desert, he [great *net*] named: *Kauisikī* (two superimposed rocks in Tahquitz Canyon from which the *Kauisiktum* clan takes its name . . ." (Strong 1929:101).

Cow nuk kal kik tem (Kaunukvela) (36)

Near Baptista (six miles northwest of Anza), on the south side of Thomas Mountain. Near present-day Ramona Reservation (Patencio 1943:113).

This was the original home of the *Kaunukalkiktum*, who later moved to *Īvīatim* village (Agua Dulce). The *Īvīatim* people, possibly a collateral lineage, were subordinate to them (Strong 1929:42, 50, 57, Ftnt. 132).

Two trails shown on the 1897-98 USGS San Jacinto topographic map lead to the Ramona Reservation. One trail heads east from Tripp Flats ending near that reservation; another runs northeast from *Paui* to the south base of Thomas Mountain, ending near the south end of the Reservation. Near this latter trail a third trail, the Ramona Trail, climbs over Thomas Mountain to Garner Valley.

Cow on vah al ham ah (37)   Point Happy (Indian Wells Point)
"The sharp point of the pestle of the mortar or grinding stone" (Patencio 1943:101).

In the story of the five head men who came to the Coachella Valley, the people are said to have settled for good at the east side of this point (Patencio 1943:101).

The culture hero Eagle Flower, in another Cahuilla story, left Indian Wells, "and went on to Indian Wells Point. . . . So he stood where the cut (highway) now is, against the rock. . . . He was lying on his arm against the rock, and the marks of his arm, his ribs, his hip, were to be seen in the rock there. . . . Then he went around to the top of the hill . . . When he came to the top of the hill he made a small hole, so that he could see without being seen and he put his knees and his elbow on the rock, and leaned his chin on the edge of the hole in the rock, to see down below. . . . On the rock at the top of the hill he left the sign of his knees, his elbow and his chin" (Patencio 1943:42).

In a version of the story told by Akasem Levi, "*Aswitseī* (Eagle Flower) stopped first at Happy Point (near Indian Wells) where he left the imprint of his elbows and knees in the rock. From there he came south along the San Jacinto mountains to a place west of Toro; he was weeping and he pushed a hole in the ground with his staff which is still there" (Strong 1929:86).

Alejo Patencio told it as follows: "Then *aswitseī* came up to the mountains at *kavinic* where he leaned against a rock leaving the marks of his elbows and knees. He looked toward *maulmii* (Toro), then he climbed up the mountain and lay down watching the people, leaving the marks of his elbows and ribs. As he came down he slipped leaving the print of his hand in the soft rocks. Near *kavinic* was a palm with which he talked" (Strong 1929: 102).

"The eagle *Aswetsei* was the mythical leader of the *Sewakil* clan of the coyote moiety. In the mountains to the west of Coachella is a rock where this deity rested. The marks in the rock show the position of his chin, elbows, and feet. The marks of his feet have been damaged by white people" (Gifford 1918:188-189).

"The Indian people have the history of only three times that the ocean came into this valley. The water always stopped a few miles west of Indian Wells Point" (Patencio 1943:83).

Cow wis to lek ets (38)   Unnamed Point, Palm Canyon Wash
"Black rock"   East of Andreas Canyon
"Now *Evon ga net* was all this time laying out sections of land for different tribes of his people. He came to the first point which he named *Cow wis to lek ets* . . ." (Patencio 1943:53).

Schwenn notes that the western edge of the Murray Hills (Santa Rosa foothills) has three points--the first, south of Andreas Cove, the second, north of Andreas Cove, and the third at Palm Canyon wash and Highway 111. She identifies "Black Rock" as the first point north of the mouth of Palm Canyon and Hermit's Bench, opposite (due east) of the mouth of Andreas Canyon on the edge of Palm Canyon wash.

Coyote Canyon (193)

See Rockhouse Valley.

Coyote Creek (Anza-Borrego State Park) (39)

In the immediate precontact period, five lineages of the *Wiwaiistam* clan lived in Coyote Canyon. One of these was the *Sauicpakiktum* in the Thousand Palms Canyon off Collins Valley. It moved from there to Rockhouse Canyon and some of its members subsequently move to the Torres-Martinez area. There has been a great deal of going back and forth from these places to Coyote Canyon, however (Strong 1929; Reed 1963; Merriam field notes; Bean filed notes). See the discussion of the Santa Rosa and Rockhouse Canyon areas.

Coyote Creek is the only year-round running stream in San Diego County and along the south escarpment of the Santa Rosa Mountains. The Creek supports several riparian areas, including the Lower Willows and the Middle Willows.

Dead Indian Creek Palms (40)

This is a palm oasis in Dead Indian Canyon at the confluence of Ebbens, Grapevine, and Dead Indian Creek just west of where the Art Smith trail leaves the main canyon. Dead Indian Creek empties into Carrizo Creek (Henderson 1961:25). Katherine Saubel says that Pedro Chino hunted there, and that it may have been a place of residual power (Jeffrey 1991).

Devil Canyon (41)

This canyon drains an area along the east flank of Sheep Mountain, emptying into Guadalupe Canyon near its mouth. The lower canyon, known as Lost Canyon, supports a palm oasis and can be reached by a trail from Guadalupe Canyon; the upper Canyon, by the main trail between La Quinta and Cactus Springs. The lower canyon was easily accessible to Cahuilla living at *Toro*, upper La Quinta, and other places.

Devil's Garden (42)

The Devil's Garden is an area which contains a wider variety of cactus species than perhaps any other equivalent area of this size in the American Southwest. These species range from the miniature *Mamillaria* to the large *Opuntias* and *Echinocactus*, including the barrel cactus, which rivals the giant *Sahuro* in size. Creosote bushes are interspersed among the cacti (James 1918:477).

Dos Palmas Spring (West Fork, Palm Canyon) (43)

This Dos Palmas spring is on the Cahuilla Trail that runs between Hermit's Bench (Palm Canyon) and Agua Fuerte Spring, south of the west fork of Palm Canyon. Palms grow at the spring and wild horses frequent the area near the spring. Petroglyphs are located across the canyon from the spring.

Dos Palmas Spring (Carrizo Creek) (44)

A spring near the source of Carrizo Creek, which flows into the desert east of Cahuilla Hills and into the Palm Desert area. The spring is near the trail from Palm Desert to Pinyon Flat and there probably was a branch trail that led to it. It was probably the site of a palm oasis.

Dos Palmas (East shore, Salton Sea) (45)

There was a place for training of young shamans at Dos Palmas (U.S. Department of the Interior, Bureau of Land Management, Ethnographic Notes 22, 1978). Because the site discussed there is a hot spring, we are inclined to believe that yet another Dos Palmas, the one on the east shore of the Salton Sea is the one referred to.

Ebbens Creek (46)

This creek and Grapevine Creek join with Dead Indian Creek, which, with Carrizo Creek, empty onto the desert south of Palm Desert. These creeks provided a water supply for an important hunting area. A series of Palm Oases are located along the creek near the old Cahuilla Trail between the mouth of Palm Canyon and Deep Canyon.

Echo Cliffs (42)

The Echo Cliffs, mentioned by Patencio in connection with the occupation of the mouth of Tahquitz Canyon by the Fox Tribe who are ancestral to the Palm Springs Indians (1943:73) are the shear cliffs on the southeast side of Tahquitz Creek just east of the canyon mouth and gaging station. The best place to hear and generate echoes is from the stream terrace on the opposite side of the creek.

Ēit (48)   Murray Canyon
"Thief"

Ēit was the name given Murray Canyon by the "great *net*" (Strong 1929:100; Bean field notes).

Eng be cha (Iñvitca) (49)   Fern Canyon
"Salt spring"

"This spring furnished salt for the people when they did not go to the Salton Sea for it" (Patencio 1943:97).

This is the small canyon behind the water tank and just north of the mouth of Tahquitz Canyon. It appears as a green spot on the mountain side just west of Tahquitz. This canyon's local name, Fern Canyon, is not shown on the maps. It should not be confused with Wentworth Canyon which because of its maidenhair ferns is also known locally as Fern Canyon.

Ēova (50)

Ēova is described as a locality due west of Alamo. This would place it in Martinez Canyon, probably on the south fork. The terrace there contains numerous cactus, agave, cholla, etc. Two trails led up onto the terrace, one from each end. Three lineages, the *Palpūnivikiktum*, the *Tamulañitcum*, and the *Tēviñakiktum*--all living at *Palpūnivikiktum hemki*--gathered cactus, spring and summer at *Ēova*, which was regarded as their original clan home. The descendants of these groups still live on Martinez Reservation (Strong 1929:50).

E pah **(51)**   Eagle Canyon & Spring
"To drink"

    The culture hero *Evon ga net* "then found what is now Eagle Canyon and the Springs which he named *E pah* . . ." (Patencio 1943:53).

    Schwenn notes that Eagle Canyon is not labeled on the USGS topo, but its mouth (where Wessman has his construction yard) is at the back of Midway Plaza in Palm Springs just west of the trailer park in Section 32, T4S, R5E. The spring is located in the north fork at about 800' above sea level (ASL). It contains a stand of native fan palms. Eagle Canyon should not be confused with the other Eagle Canyon, *Os Wit* Canyon, the large canyon between Tahquitz and Andreas Canyons.

E va we **(52)**   One Horse Point
"The wind blows all the time"

    After the culture hero *Evon ga net* crossed Snow Creek, "he went to another point which had a spring of water. He called this place *E va we* . . ." (Patencio 1943: 54).

    On this point *Evon ga net* threw away the wild wheat he had gathered in the sand hills, "and to this time wild bunches of this wheat grow there" (Patencio 1943:54).

    Schwenn notes that there are two points west of Snow Creek--the first is at the west end of the mouth of Snow Creek Canyon and the second, about two miles farther west. One Horse Spring is located about 1 mile south of the second point. The second point has, as far as is known, no local name and is unnamed on the USGS topographic maps; so it is named here for the spring. It is assumed that this is the point referred to above.

Fat mel mo **(53)**
"A place among many hills"

    Traveling down Palm Canyon from Indian Potrero to the Garden of Eden, the culture hero *Evon ga net* "named *Fat mel mo* in Palm Canyon. . . ." (Patencio 1943:53).

    Schwenn believes that the area described could be on the east side of Palm Canyon and the Palm Canyon Trail, either just to the south of Dry Rock Wash or between the wash and the Murray Hills (Santa Rosa foothills), i.e., in the headwaters of the East Fork of Palm Canyon just south of Hermit's Bench.

"Fig Tree John" Petroglyphs (54)

    Steward describes a group of petroglyphs at "Point Fig Tree John" near the road along the ancient shore of Lake Cahuilla. They are carved into travertine, apparently before the last rise of Lake Cahuilla and were subsequently inundated. The travertine is composed of the shells of barnacle-like animals. The rock art is both carved and painted (1929:84-85).

Fish Trap Petroglyphs (55)

    These petroglyphs are close to the ancient Cahuilla fish traps. Native Americans in the area consider them "national treasures," as a symbols of their sacred past. They should be nominated for the National Register of Historic Places in order to be adequately protected and preserved.

Fish Traps (56)

"The water left a great salt lake in the valley . . . With the water came fish" (Patencio 1943:83).

"Then it was that the Indians began to make traps to catch fish. They made the traps in the rocks. . ..The Indians used nets in them."

"These traps are along different places down the Coachella Valley and Imperial Valley, but not at all places, only at the places where the Indians could have trails leading down to the traps" (Patencio 1943:84).

Akasem Levi and Francisco Nombre told Strong that the 'fish traps' west of Martinez formerly belonged to the *Awilem* clan on the basis of clan oral history (Strong 1929:97,Ftnt.). These fish traps are located west of the intersection of Jackson Street and Avenue 66, west of Valerie Jean's and Highway 86.

Along what was the falling shoreline of ancient Lake Cahuilla lie a series of fish traps made of rocks, that were built by the Cahuilla four or five hundred years ago. When the Colorado River changed its course, the huge freshwater lake began to dry up, a process that took fifty to sixty years, according to modern estimates. When the lake became too saline to support the growth of fish, these died by the thousands, and the Cahuilla built the fish traps to catch them as the waters receded. The experience lived on in their oral history. Although many scholars ignored these oral traditions, work by Dr. Phillip Wilke (1976:178-180) confirmed their use as fish traps and demonstrated the significance of those in Cahuilla economic history.

Another set of fish traps are located along the old lake shore (Lake Cahuilla) near Travertine point. Near these are weirs.

Gash mo (57)

"The sound of the crunching of sand as one walks"

The culture hero *Evon ga net* went down Palm Canyon "until he came to what once was called 'The Garden of Eden,' to the east side of it. That place he called *Gash mo*" (Patencio 1943:53).

Schwenn points out that for the sound of crunching sand one must be in or near a wash, in this case, probably near the confluence of Andreas and Palm Canyon washes.

The Garden of Eden was in the eastern part of Section 35. It was one of the first land development schemes in Palm Springs. B. B. Barney started selling five to twenty acre tracts there in early 1888, but the project failed after the long drought that began in 1894. He irrigated it with water from Andreas Canyon, which the Cahuilla had used to water their lands in Section 2 to the south before Barney took over the water.

Gordon Trail (58)

This trail follows an aboriginal trail climbing from the mouth of Andreas Canyon along the ridge between Andreas and *Os wit* Canyons to join the trail out of Tahquitz and continue to Caramba and then onto San Jacinto [71-T8]. It was also called the Palms to Pines Trail (Patencio 1943:71,90). At Caramba there are yellow pine and oak woodlands, plus bedrock mortar sites.

The trail should not be confused with another aboriginal trail, also known as the Palms To Pines Trail, which climbs from the mouths of Dead Indian and Carrizo Canyons in Palm Desert to Pinyon Flats (See Carrizo Creek entry). Present-day Highway 74 follows the route of the latter trail.

Guadalupe Creek (59)

This creek runs down a canyon from the Santa Rosa Mountains, having its source on Martinez Mountain. It flows into the desert three or four miles northwest of *Toro*, coming out in the same place as Devil's Canyon.

Ha much cha vis ba **(60)**   San Gorgonio Pass

"Place where there were so many people, they closed up our getting through" (Patencio 1943:100).

The pass that Cahuillas under five head men went through when entering the Coachella Valley. Eagle Flower is also said to have come through the pass (Patencio 1943:100,42).

The San Gorgonio Pass was the territory of the *Wanakik* Cahuilla clan, the lineages of which occupied canyon mouths opening out from both sides (Bean 1960).

This pass is and has always been extremely important as the most convenient pass between the Colorado Desert areas through the intervening mountains to the Los Angeles Basin. Indian trails converged here just as roads, railroad tracks, and transmission lines do today.

Hauiñenin **(61)**

One of three large rocks near the south point of Chino Canyon named by the great *net* (Strong 1929:101).

Hauĩtalal **(62)**

The second of three large rocks near the south point of Chino Canyon named by the great *net* (Strong 1929:101).

Haviñavitcum Territory **(63)**   Palm Springs Station

The *Haviñavitcum* (Gifford 1918:191) or *Havina Wanakik* (Bean 1960:112), a lineage of the *Wanakik* Cahuilla, lived at Palm Springs Station in the early 19th century. Although they had their homes down on the desert they used the Santa Rosa Mountains for hunting, gathering, and various ceremonial events.

Hermit's Bench Palm Oasis (64)

The largest number of *Washingtonia filifera* fan palms in the United States occurs in Palm Canyon just south of the bench. Currently the bench is the location of the Trading Post in Andreas Canyon (Henderson 1941:26).

Hiawat **(65)**

A ridge in the Santa Rosa Mountains. According to Chase, Cahuilla leader Juan Razon ("Fig Tree John") showed him an aged document in which the great Cahuilla chief Cabezon had appointed Razon as Capitan of Agua Dulce *Tuba* village, and owner of all the territory "running from the last low ridge of the Santa Rosas (the ridge was named *Hiawat* on the map . . .) as far as Conejo Prieto or Black Rabbit [now Rabbit] Peak" (Chase 1919:182).

Hidden Gulch Palms (66)

This palm oasis lies on a trail at the foot of Murray Hill back of Palm Springs. It would have been used by people hunting and gathering in the Murray Hill area (Henderson 1961). These are probably the palms that grow in the canyon north of Andreas Cove and west of the Theleman Trail.

Hidden Spring (Anza-Borrego State Park) (67)

A spring at Jackass Flat in Rockhouse Canyon, near which lies the site if the village of *Ataki* (Bean field notes 1960; Reed 1963:120). It should not to be confused with the Hidden Springs in the Mecca Hills, described under *Kawis-pa-miya*.

Hōkwitca (68)

Clan home of the *Hōkwitcakiktum* clan, Wildcat moiety, before they moved to *Wiasmul*.
Its probable location was on the flat just north of the head of the Middle Fork of Borrego Palm Canyon (Strong 1929:145, 148).

Ho-la-kal (Hulaqal) (69)   San Ysidro
"Wild buckwheat" (*Eriogonum fasciculatum*) (Bean and Saubel 1972:72).
The home of the *Wilakal* people, according to Strong, a hybrid group composed linguistically in the 1920s of Cahuilla, Cupeño, and Diegueño families in about equal numbers" (Strong 1929:146). According to Gifford, San Ysidro was the home of the *Wiyistam* clan of the Coyote clan. Gifford noted that the *Wakwaikiktum* clan, Wildcat moiety, appeared "to have come from the same region" (Gifford 1918:191).

Hoon wit ten ca va (70)   Garnet Hill
"Hills of the roasted bear"
The Cahuilla culture hero *Ca wis ke on ca*, naming sites in *Kauisik* territory, went from the mouth of Eagle Canyon to the Garnet Hills [sic], which he "named the Hills of the Roasted Bear" (Patencio 1943:99). It should be noted that the Cahuilla revered the bear, which was not a food for them.

Horse Potrero Canyon ("Potrero Canyon" on newer 7.5 minute topos) (71)

This is a tributary of Palm Canyon near Agua Bonita Spring. Horse Canyon, a tributary of Coyote Canyon, was a connecting link with the Los Coyotes area. It has a long history of occupation and use by the Cahuilla (Reed 1963). The village *Tatmilmi* may have been near Horse Portero.

Hou wit s sa ke (72)
"A bear-skin blanket"
The Cahuilla culture hero *Ca wis ke on ca*, naming sites in *Kauisik* territory, "crossed the valley to the sand wash, near the mouth of Eagle Canyon, and he called the place *Hou wit s sa ke*, meaning a bear-skin blanket" (Patencio 1943:99). This passage does not imply that the Cahuilla killed bears to acquire blankets.

Hunavatikiktum Village (73)   Hall's Grade

The *Hunavatikiktum* in Hall's Grade, San Gorgonio Pass (Gifford 1918:191). This group was the *Huvana* lineage of the *Wanakik* Cahuilla (Bean 1960).

Hunwit hekik (74)   Long Valley
"Place of the bear"

A grassy cienega on Tahquitz Creek that marked the northern boundary of the territory belonging to the *Paniktum* lineage of Andreas Canyon (Strong 1929:101).

Ilwukwinet (75)   Coyote Canyon

Place in Los Coyotes Canyon that was the original home of the *Masūwitcem* and the *Mūmlētcem*, both Coyote moiety (Strong 1929:42, 51).

Indian Spring (76)

This spring near Dos Palmas Spring (in Palm Canyon), provided an important source of water for the West Fork of Palm Canyon. The nearby flat may be *Kalahal* (Strong 1929:100).

Ish el wat tow ta um ali (78)
"Coyote digging"

A low piece of land back of Palm Springs, named by the culture hero *Ca Wis ke on ca*, about a mile beyond the boundary sign, which is about a half mile beyond the first old reservoir at the south point of Chino Canyon. It is near where Highway 111 takes a turn. The plant, *Mes sal em*, was gathered in the spring down the wash and across the boulevard from "the coyote digging." *Mesalem* was a plant like asparagus with sweet potato-type roots (Patencio 1943:99). "*Mes sal em*" may be identical to "*Mis-a-lem*" or "*Meslam*," identified by Bean and Saubel as *Orobanche ludoviciana* (1972:97).

Īsilsiveyaiutcem (79)
"Rock basin for Coyote's water"

A place in Martinez Canyon, exact location unknown, where the *Wantcinakiktum* moved after leaving *Pūichekiva*. It may have been their original home (Strong 1929:41,45). This is the lineage name of the Siva family.

Isil kaw-we-vah-ah (77)   Coyote Mortar Rock

One of two large rocks, near *Num na sh b al*, "Place Of Resting" rock, that have small mortar holes in them, not more than three inches across. These small holes were never used for grinding, but to make the sign of the trail. Coyote mortar rock has the deeper hole. "The other is called the wild cat mortar rock . . ." (Patencio 1943:98).

"In going up Chino Canyon he made the sign of the trails. Going hunting to the top of the mountains, he put the marks on the rocks" (Patencio 1943:96).

Num na sh b al stands by the old Cahuilla trail from Palm Springs to Chino Canyon near the boundary sign on the south point of Chino Canyon.

Īva (80)   Gilman's Hot Springs

A hot spring just north of Soboba where the great *net* moved his people from Redlands Junction (Strong 1929:100).

Deputy Surveyor Henry Hancock described the springs in late August-early September, 1867, as "at the base of the Mountain is a swamp with springs now called Cienega del Aqua Caliente" (Record Book 30:50).

Ívawakik (81)   Cabezon Hill

Sharp hill south of the city of Cabezon that was named by the great *net*, who went inside of the hill and became the rock on top of it that marks the northeastern boundary of *Kauisik* Cahuilla territory (Strong 1929:101).

Ívĩatim (82)

Ívĩatim was a Cahuilla Village at the site of a warm spring near present-day Oasis. The vicinity was known as Agua Dulce earlier in this century. It was the home of the *Kaunukalkiktum* ("living at *kaunukvela*") clan and of its subsidiary *Ívĩatim* lineage. The *Kaunukalkiktum* had seven houses there at one time, including the home of a religious and political leader or *net* (a ceremonial house). The *Ívĩatim*, who also had seven houses, shared the *net* of the *Kaunukalkiktum* at the earliest period remembered by Strong's informant Francisco Nombre, but may have been an older lineage rather than a branch of the clan.

The houses of the two groups were on either side of the spring, which was in the center of the village. The area to the west of the spring is where the people from the village carried on hunting, gathering, and ceremonial activities (Strong 1929:39,42,50).

I was wa ba all (83)
"The place of grinding [meal or flour]"
A small, otherwise unnamed, canyon between Eagle Canyon and Song Point, about 0.7 mile east of Song Point on Hwy 111, visited by culture hero *Evon ga net* while establishing tribal boundaries (Patencio 1943:53).

Jackass Flat (84)

Jackass Flat is the site of Hidden Spring (*Ataki*). Rockhouse Canyon connects Jackass Flat and Rockhouse Valley. Jackass Flat was therefore an important occupation area.

Juan Razon's Allotment (85)

This forty acres in Section 28, Township 8 south, R. 9 east, was the allotment of Juan Razon, "Fig Tree John" (Beidler 1977).

Kakwawit (86)   Tahquitz Canyon, Mouth Of

The great *net* gave this name of the mouth of Tahquitz Canyon back of Palm Springs (Strong 1929:101).

Part of the *Kauisiktum* lineage occupied the mouth of Tahquitz canyon as late as the nineteenth century. See Bean and Vane's report on the Tahquitz Project, to be published in 1991.

The waterfall not far up the canyon from its mouth is a famous tourist site. As late as the 1920s, Palm Springs youngsters, Cahuilla and non-Indians alike, enjoyed swimming in the pool at its base.

The canyon in its upper reaches is very steep. Many of those who have accepted the challenge of climbing up Tahquitz Canyon have come to grief, a number of them suffering fatal falls.

Kakwawit, the Mouth of Tahquitz Canyon

In this picture, probably taken early in the twentieth century, we look up into Tahquitz Canyon from a pasture that was undoubtedly watered by the water from Tahquitz Canyon. The City of Palm Springs now reaches all the way to the road that can be seen beyond the fence.

Kalahal (87)

This flat northwest of Indian Potrero named by the great *net* cannot be definitely identified, but could be either Bullseye Flat or an unnamed flat in the West Fork near Indian Spring (Strong 1929:101).

Kauissimtcem hemki̅ (89)

This is a small semi-circular hill just south of Andreas Creek at the base of the mountains that was the sacred hillock where the Cahuilla landed when they first flew to Palm Canyon. The hill is just to the east of the trail from the Andreas Palms picnic area and the mouth of Murray Canyon about 0.1 miles south of the parking area. Alejo Patencio tells of the great *net* naming it (Strong 1929:101).

Kauistanalmū (90)

The third of three large rocks near the south point of Chino Canyon named by the great *net* (Strong 1929:101).

Kaukwicheki (91)

The great *net*, while marking the territory of the *Kauisik*, named a stream north and west of Palm Canyon where hunters and acorn gatherers camped "*Kaukwicheki*" (Strong 1929:100). It seems likely that Apache Spring is the source of this stream.

Kawis Ah-mov-vash (92)   Hunter's Rock

"Then there is a small rock on the trail below in the canyon, just before coming to the point, where offerings were placed. This rock is by the old deep-worn Indian trail going from Palm Springs to Chino Canyon. . . . This is the hunter's rock. The hunters put their offerings there, and then never get tired or bitten by animals or snakes, or frightened" (Patencio 1943:72).

Hunter's Rock is located at the south point of Chino Canyon in the canyon below Leaning Rock. Nearby, also along the old Cahuilla trail, is another small rock, the "Place Of Resting" Rock, and near the later rock are the Coyote and Wildcat Mortar Rocks (Patencio 1943:98). On the hillside above is the Leaning Rock and across from it, Hoof Of The Rock and Thundering Rock (Patencio 1943:72-73).

Kawishmu (94)

This small hill east of Whitewater Canyon, possibly Whitewater Hill, marks the boundary between the Desert Cahuilla and the *Wanupiapayum* of the San Gorgonio Pass. According to Kroeber, this is the Serrano place name (1908:35).

Kawish-wa-wat-acha (93)
From *Qawish*, "the rock," and *Wavu'-wet*, "tall" (Barrows 1900; Bright 1967:xxiv).

A water hole in the San Jacinto Mountains where the birds came to drink: "Now, because there was no water at any other place, all the birds and animals came to the Mockingbird's water hole to drink. . . . the Mockingbird did not like this. . . . the birds left the water hole and went away to the San Jacinto Mountains. There they found the rain and there was snow. They had nothing to eat and they were very cold. They looked down on the other side and saw a valley. It was not raining there. It looked pretty and green. So, they decided to go down into it. From there they went to the coast and decided to settle there" (Patencio 1971:31). This text is from one of the Cahuilla song cycles called "bird songs" which recount various events in Cahuilla prehistory. These songs are still sung.

Kawis-pa-miya (95)   Mecca Hills Village
"Rock water hold" (Curtis 1926:163)

Possibly another name for *Maswut Helaanut*, a village in Painted Canyon that was the home of the *Kauwicpamēauitcem* clan, of which Cabezon was chief (Strong 1929:53).

Schwenn notes that Curtis gives the location as north of Mecca, however Curtis' directions are suspect as he states, for example, that Indian Wells is southwest of Indio. Indian Wells is actually west of Indio. Therefore at a guess this location is northeast to east of Mecca. The two most likely locations are Painted, Box, and Hidden Springs Canyons. There is a natural spring with some 31 adult *Washingtonia filifera* palms and 27 seedling palms in a narrow defile off the central fork of Hidden Springs Canyon. Several trails lead from Box Canyon to this location. Down Hidden Springs Canyon about one-half mile is a small side canyon with 5 struggling palms and a seep, known both as Burnt Palms and Sheep Hole Oasis. One of the trails from Box Canyon passes this location on its way to Hidden Springs.

Kekliva (96)

A mountain just north of *Saboba* to which the great *net* took his people after they left *Iva*. The *Kauisiktum* left part of their ceremonial bundle at *Kekliva* (Strong 1929:100).

Kelewutkwiikwinut (Ekwawinet) (97)
"Wood hanging down"

The original name of the village of *Iltcuñaloñi* lineage, which was west of the highway at La Mesa. This was the home of the *Sēwahilem* lineage, Coyote moiety, and the *Telkiktum* lineage, Wildcat moiety (Strong 1929:52).

Key wat wah he wen e (98)
"A dividing line"
A "sign" placed by the culture hero *Ca wis ke on ca* at a place "about one half mile beyond the first old reservoir [one of the several water tanks along the south end of Chino Drive in Palm Springs]. There he put the sign which gave to him the land between that place and Whitewater Point. The land was given him by his people, for his own home." This sign was close to a table-like rock which stands by the old Indian trail, *Num na sh b al*, and is probably on the South Point, Chino Canyon (Patencio 1943:98).

Kick ke san lem mo (99)

"The place where the white flowers [probably *Datura metaloides*] grow." A place named by culture hero *Ca wis ke on ca* when marking the boundaries of *Kawisik* territory. It is described as "about a mile up the wash, west" from the mouth of Eagle Canyon (Patencio 1943:99). It is located where the Palm Canyon and Tahquitz Washes join.

Kish chowl (Kistacavel) (100)
"Sharp pointed house roofs"
Sharp pointed rocks north of Palm Springs. From a place in Whitewater Wash where there were two desert willows, *Evon ga net* "crossed the valley again south, and came to those jagged red rocks which still stand alone by the side of the highway" (Patencio 1943:54).

The great *net*, travelling north "named...*Kistacavel* (at point where second bridge on highway from Palm Springs to Whitewater is located)." (Strong 1929:101).

Schwenn notes that the second bridge is probably the first bridge (going east only) about one mile west of Tramway Drive. This bridge spans the Chino Canyon wash near the north point of the canyon. The jagged rocks are located on the south of Hwy 111 in the mouth of Chino Canyon about 1.35 miles northwest of Tramway Drive and very close to the second bridge.

Kiwil (Kēwil) (101)   Old Santa Rosa

A village near Cottonwood Spring in the fork of Rockhouse Canyon whose ruins can still be seen. This village was occupied in the late 19th century by families of the *Sauicpakiktum* lineage, who had moved there from Los Coyotes sometime prior to the smallpox epidemic of the 1860s. At an earlier time it was occupied by the *Wantciñakik-tamianawitcem*, who moved from there to *Tuva* (Strong 1929:41,146, 151).

At this site are three rock houses, the largest about 15 feet square, spaced along an elongated ridge southeast of the Cottonwood Springs. "The water source for this settlement was said to be a spring next to a lone cottonwood tree 0.1 mile east. Both the tree and the spring seem to have been victims of the tropical storms of the late 70s; only a dry, sandy wash is in evidence there today." The "Cottonwood Springs indicated on USGS topo maps northwest of the ruins is apparently in error" (Schad 1986:196-197).

Kolwovakut (102)   Old Santa Rosa Village

One of two villages in Rock House Canyon. Schwenn believes it was probably located about the second of two seeps at the base of the Santa Rosa Mountains east of the mouth of Nicolias Canyon. The first seep is located at 4200 feet in a canyon (Section 17) and had mortars and ollas (removed years ago); the second seep, covered with mesquite, is at 3920 feet in Section 18.

"Obscure trails radiate from the old village to all parts of the valley. At least two, still traceable, ascend ridgelines about one mile east-southeast of the village and connect with a trail into Martinez Canyon . . ." (Schad 1984:198).

Some suggest that Old Santa Rosa was actually in Nicholias Canyon. See "Nicholias Canyon Village" entry.

Konkistū-uinut (103)

"Going southeast from Murray Hill" the great *net*, in the course of tracing the boundaries of *Kauisik* territory, "named . . . *konkistū-uinut* (a place near Indian Wells . . . .") near the southeastern boundary of the territory (Strong 1929:101).

Konkistū-uinut is probably in the vicinity of Haystack Mountain and the drainage divide between Magnesia Spring and Cat Canyons.

Kōtevewit (104)

The village of *Kōtevewit* was located in a valley with water, about five miles south of Point Happy and a short distance from the present La Quinta Hotel. The culture hero *Aswitsei*, Eagle Flower, went there and lived for many years (Patencio 1943:43).

"Then he [*Aswitsei*, Eagle Flower] settled at *kōtevewit* (in the mountains) . . . A man named *kauicwikil* lived near there on the edge of the desert . . . [and] had a beautiful young daughter . . . He [*Aswitsei*] married her and stayed at *kōtevewit*" (Strong 1929:86).

The La Quinta Hotel is located at 49-499 Eisenhower, La Quinta. From Washington, turn west onto Eisenhower and left (south) where Eisenhower curves to the second right after the curve (about a quarter mile). This site would have been close to the shoreline of ancient Lake Cahuilla when the lake was at its maximum size. The shoreline at the high stand of the lake reached to the south point of La Quinta cove.

Kow wish so kalet (105)   Rock on Cabazon Peak (4551')

"The rock sign in which lives this man *Evon ga net*, the fox" (Patencio 1943:54).

"Then he passed into this mountain forever. He came out away up at the top as a great white rock that is in the shape of a dome on the top of the mountain. The dome is seen from Whitewater to Cabazon from the boulevard" (Patencio 1943:54).

Kow wish so kalet is an enormous rock near the summit of Cabezon Peak, which is just south of Cabazon and resembles a big head.

Kūpa (Ko-pa) (106)   Agua Caliente
"To drink or swallow"   Warner Hot Springs
In the mid-nineteenth century, the home of the *Sauivilem*, who came there from *Sauivil*. They were a lineage of the *Wiwaiistam* clan (Strong 1929:146, 148).

According to oral history, Yellow Body or *Takweltekesnikish* came there at a time when there was no water there. He "took a great basket which he set in the spring. He made his mother, his wife, and his dog get into the basket. Then he got in himself, and causing the basket to whirl like a wheel, they all sank into the spring forever" (Patencio 1943:39-40). See also Hooper 1920:374-376.

Kwa-le-ki (107)
Probably from *Qwa-al heki'*, "hawk's home," from *Qwa'al*, "hawk," and *Heki'*, "his home" "house."

This is the site of a small village at Pinyon Flats described by Barrows (1900:27): "These villages seem to have been halfway camps between the desert and mountain rancherias farther on, and probably never more than a few families occupied them at a time. The elevation is five of six thousand feet higher than the desert, and the air is bracing and fine."

Cahuilla elder Alice Lopez was not familiar with the name *Kwa-le-ki*, but said there was a camping place at Pinyon Flat where they used to stop when they went to Santa Barbara (Vane field notes, 1979). There was a Cahuilla settlement at Santa Barbara (Johnson 1990).

Lake Cahuilla, Ancient Salton Sea (108)

Cahuilla oral literature recalls rather accurately the history of this body of water as revealed by archaeological studies:

"The Indian people have the history of only three times that the ocean came into this valley. The water always stopped a few miles west of Indian Wells Point. . . .we know that when it [the water] came, it came quick, with a sound, a roar, that was heard much distance away. . . .The water left a great salt lake in the valley for much time before it dried up. With the water came fish" (Patencio 1943:83).

"We do not know, only that the water came three times. The third and last time it came slowly. All the Indian people knew that it was coming. They sent fast runners for all the head men, all the medicine men, all the men of power to come. They gathered together everyone of them, and they used their power as they went to meet it. The water stopped. It never came again. But a lake was left in the middle of the Valley for much time. Then it dried up and went away" (Patencio 1943: 84-85).

The ancient shoreline of Lake Cahuilla which can be seen up from the present shoreline of the Salton Sea that now fills some of the same basin, was an aboriginal hunting and gathering area (Romero 1954; Wilke 1976:22).

La-wil-van (Sivel) (109)   Alamo (Alamo Bonito)
"Cottonwood," and "sycamore," respectively.

These two names were given by Barrows for the village at Alamo (1900:34; Bright 1967:xxv).

According to Gifford, the village was occupied by the *Walpunidikiktum*, Wildcat moiety (Gifford 1918:190). Strong suggests that Barrows applied these names to *Palpunivikiktum hemki* and states that his informants did not remember either of these names (Strong, Ftnt 123, p. 50, 1929).

Alamo Bonito Springs, no longer shown on the USGS topos, was located near the corner of Avenue 74 and Pierce in Section 35, T7S, R8E, SBBM. There were a group of artesian springs at this site. Alamo Bonito is Spanish for "pretty popular," referring in this case to the cottonwood. The village was visited by Frances Anthony (1901:26) and later by Chase (1919:176). At the time of Chase's visit the "capitan" was Jake Razonas (Jake Razon).

This site would have been about 184 feet below sea level. At its high stand ancient Lake Cahuilla rose to 40 feet above sea level.

Lincoln Peak (110)

The culture hero *Ca wis ke on ca*, marking the boundaries of *Kauisik* territory, "came down what is now Tahquitz Canyon. . . . Then he climbed the hill we called Lincoln Peak" (Patencio 1943:97).

Abe Lincoln Peak is shown on the northwest side of Tahquitz Canyon, elev. 3830' on USGS 1897-98 USGS topo; while not named on the current USGS Palm Springs 7.5-min topo, Abe Lincoln is the peak west of Tahquitz Canyon, elev. 3808'.

Little Clark Lake (111)

There were acres in this dry lake where water was close enough to the surface to support large areas of mesquite growth. Hence this was a mesquite gathering place for the Cahuilla, who would come to the mesquite groves each season. Antelope and various small game animals and birds were hunted in the area (Bean field notes, ca. 1960).

Mad Woman Spring (112)

This spring, now part of the Agua Caliente Reservation, is more a dripping seep than a spring.

Magnesia Spring (113)

This spring is the source of water in Magnesia Spring Canyon, *Pah-wah-te.*

Mala (114)   Chino Canyon Village Site

Curtis gives *Mala* as the name of a village "at the base of San Jacinto peak in a canon west of Agua Caliente" (1926:164). Patencio says that the summer home of the Palm Springs Indians was in Chino Canyon. "There we had good land . . . for fields and gardens" (Patencio 1943:56).

Francisco Patencio, who was born in Chino Canyon, says that his people had fields and gardens there, irrigated by an open water ditch at first and then by a stone lined ditch, made by the grandfathers and great grandfathers of the tribe. It began at the cave where he played as a boy and went down the canyon for two miles.

There was a hot spring in which the children bathed at in the riparian area.

"One time the people had their things all packed up to come down into the valley below . . . Then (I was alive, but very small) my people saw a great white cloud rising over San Jacinto Mountain. It was coming very fast . . . the thunder and lightning began coming, then rain and wind. . . . The floods began roaring down the canyons. My people only had time to catch up their children and rush up the mountain side to save their lives. When the waters from the cloud-burst had passed on, everything had gone with it. The homes of my people and all they had were gone forever. . . . all the good land, it was gone, too. . . . there were only piles of great rocks and washed-out gorges. My people never tried to raise anything there anymore" (Patencio 1943:56-57). This may have been the same flood that caused the *Wanikik* Cahuilla to move from Whitewater Canyon to Malki.

"Sometime after 1825 the Black Measles spread through the San Gorgonio Pass toward Palm Springs. Andres Lucero "who was looked upon by all Indians as the possessor of the greatest knowledge of botanical medicine," recalled the 1825 smallpox epidemic and the compounded herb steam baths that were used to combat it. He summoned all of his people to a large cave in Chino Canyon that had formerly been used for religious purposes and converted it into a cave-hospital. He applied his medical knowledge and saved many lives (Romero 1954:3).

Places in the Cahuilla Landscape: An Alphabetical Arrangement

A Tule House in Chino Canyon

The Kauisik Cahuilla farmed in the flatlands high in Chino Canyon fairly early in the nineteenth century. These flatlands in the canyon had the advantage that they could not be seen from the valley. They were often a place of refuge from the Spanish.

Malal (115)   Metate Point
"Metate"   North Point, Chino Canyon

The great *net*, marking the boundary of *Kauisiktum* territory and going northward "named . . . *malal* (north point of Chino Canyon) . . ." (Strong 1929:101).

This is the first point along Highway 111 west of Tramway Drive near the first bridge. The first bridge spans the Chino Canyon wash about one mile west of Tramway Drive.

Mal-ki (116)   Morongo Reservation

Malki was the territory of the *Wanikik* lineage of the *Wanikiktum* ("running water") clan, Coyote moiety, who had previously lived at Whitewater Canyon (Bean and Mason 1962; Strong 1929:91). *Malki* territory became the Potrero Indian Reservation in 1877. It is now known as the Morongo Indian Reservation. The name is preserved in that of the *Malki* Museum, which is a Cahuilla Museum on the reservation.

Martinez Canyon (117)

Schwenn identifies Martinez Canyon as the "Rinconada" described as being west of the Martinez villages by Romero (Bean and Mason 1962:47-48). This deep canyon begins in the Flat (Large Pinyon) between Martinez and Santa Rosa Mountains.

Maswut helaanut (119)
"Ceremonial matting spreading"

The southernmost Cahuilla village east of the Southern Pacific Railroad. Strong wrote that it was located in Painted Canyon two miles northeast of Mecca (1929:41, 53-54). It was the home of the *Kauwicpauméauitcem* ("caught by the rock"), Wildcat moiety, of which Cabezon was the chief

61

(Strong 1929:41; 53-54). Other spellings include "*Ka'wis-pa-miya*" (Curtis 1926:163), *Kawispa'wiya-wichem* (Curtis 1926:164): "*Kauwispaumiyawitcem*" (Gifford 1918:190). All of these variations refer to living among rocks.

Mauit (120)

Mauit, *Sēūpa*, and *Pauī* were three villages that Strong identified as centers, probably lineage centers, of a single clan. *Mauit* was three miles southeast of *Pauī*, and was possibly in Duranso Valley. It was occupied in the 1920s (Strong 1929:147). This area is associated with the Cahuilla Indian Reservation.

Mauūlmiī (121)   *Toro* (Torres)

The site of the principal village at *Toro*, said to have been the home of the *Tamolañitcem*; and of the *Sawalakiktum*, who before that lived at La Mesa with the *Nanhaiyum*. This information is from Gifford (1918:189-191), who received it from three informants. He notes that none of the clan names they gave him corresponded with the "names of present-day Cahuilla villages listed by Dr. D. P. Barrows" (1900). The *Sawalakiktum*, therefore, were apparently the occupants of the site in the late prehistoric period.

According to Strong, the *Wakaīkiktum* ("night heron"), *Pañakauissiktum* ("water fox"), and later, the *Sēwahilem* lineages lived at *Mauulmii* in the late 1870s (Strong 1929:52). See discussion of *Toro* Canyon.

U.S. Deputy Surveyor John La Croze described *Toro* in March, 1856 as having "a number of springs of good water, around which there are several acres of good grass [and] in the same section there is an Indian village known as 'Toro's,'. . ." (Record Book 57:27). *El Torro* was a stop for both the Pony Express and the Bradshaw stage (Patencio 1943:61-62).

Mīaskalet (Me ahs cal et) (122)
"A grey top"

A white-tipped rock in Tahquitz Canyon, probably on the hillside above the entrance to the canyon.

The "great *net*, . . . coming north along the eastern edge of the mountains bordering the desert, named . . . *miaskalet* (white rock on hillside in Tahquitz Canyon) . . ." (Strong 1929:101).

Ca wis ke on ca "came down to the foothills, to the place where the water of Tahquitz turns into the Indian ditch today . . . He came to a large white-tipped rock, just above the place of the fire play. This he called *Me ahs cal et* . . ." (Patencio 1943:97). (The ditch began in the canyon mouth near the gaging station.)

The fire play was a play by Mary Austin titled "Fire." It was performed as an outdoor pageant in the 1920s under the auspices of Mr. Garnet Holmes. Cahuilla tribal members, local residents and visitors all participated. The play was performed on the rising ground at the entrance to Tahquitz Canyon (Chase 1923:51).

Millyillilikalet (123)   Andreas Creek

The great *net* took his people to "*panyik* (mouth of Andreas Canyon), on a stream called *milyillikalet* and near this place he found some painted rocks called *tekic*" (Strong 1929:100). Andreas Creek was the water source that enabled the *Paniktum* lineage who lived at *Panyik* to flourish. In the late nineteenth century, they were successfully practicing agriculture until non-Indians preempted their water supply. The pictographs on the large rock formation overlooking the mouth of Andreas Canyon are a notable feature even now. See *Paniktum hemki* (Bean and Vane 1983).

It appears that the perennial water supply may date only from the 1850s: "But one time (I was very small, I could not remember yet), there came such earthquakes as had not been known to any of the people. . . . Then it was that . . . Andreas Canyon Creek that only ran in the winter became an all year stream, as it has been since. Before the earthquakes, the only water to be had there in the summer months was from a small spring which ran always in the creek beneath the caves" (Patencio 1943:58).

Patencio is probably referring to the January 9, 1857 Fort Tejon Earthquake on the San Andreas Fault. See Tahquitz Creek.

A Woman of Mauūlmīi

This is Ailena Levi with her mesquite bean storage basket at Toro. The Levis are members of the Sēwahilem lineage, originally from Kōtevewit in the Santa Rosa mountains. The legendary foundary of this lineage of Aswitseī, Eagle flower, who left the imprint of his hands and knees in the rock at Happy Point in Indian Wells. Akasem Levi told the story of Aswitseī to Strong, who gives it in some detail (1929:86-87). Patencio gives a shorter version in his book (1943:41-44).

Mission Creek home of *Kilyiñakiktum* clan (287)

Gifford (1918:190) says that the Cahuilla *Kilyiñakiktum* lineage lived at Mission Creek, presumably before the Serrano came into the area. Bean's informants said a *Wanikik* lineage lived there (Bean field notes, 1959). The *Kilyiñakiktum* may have been a lineage of the *Wanakik* clan.

Mission Creek Trail (288)

This was an important trail for the Cahuilla and Serrano who lived in the Mission Creek area, leading up the San Bernardino Mountains. It has not been definitely identified.

Moreno Valley (289)

In or near Moreno Valley, there were several Cahuilla communities, including *Junalmanat* (near present-day Winchester), which were among the first to be affected by Spanish culture. Many of the Cahuillas who lived there were baptized at San Gabriel Mission.

According to some versions of Cahuilla migration stories, the Cahuillas came to Moreno Valley on their way to the Santa Rosa Mountains and environs:

"Now the five head men who came to Moreno Valley and brought so many people, more people than had ever been together before, began to separate" (Patencio 1943:99).

"Now, when *Evon ga net* was in Moreno, there were many people. This man *Evon ga net* was a man of much power, and chief of his people. He decided he should explore more country--mark more boundary lines for his new tribes to come" (Patencio 1943:52).

"Now when *Esel i hut* . . . was coming through from the north, he was looking around, coming to see everything in his way; he came into the Moreno country . . ." (Patencio 1943:34).

"Now, in Moreno Valley was the first gathering of a great people. There were many, many people. Many men of great power, head men, medicine men, and great chiefs, were living there. As time passed, some of them went back again. Some went south, and some west, but the men of the most power came east" (Patencio 1943:50).

Mountain Home Spring (290)

A spring on Virgin Spring trail west of Santa Rosa Spring.

Mowal (292)   Salvador Canyon

"This canyon, known to the Cahuilla Indians as *Mowal*," is named for the youngest member of the second Anza expedition, Salvador Ygnacio Linares, who was born just west of here. Salvador Canyon is not a conspicuous canyon; there are neither palm trees nor other landmarks near the entrance to distinguish it from a score of other side canyons. But within its steep, narrow, verdant gorge are the many palms that once earned it the name of Thousand Palms Canyon, so referenced by Randall Henderson . . . . Henderson once counted 360 palms within the main canyon and its forks (Lindsay and Lindsay 1984:92).

Mow it check mow win it (291)   Cornell Peak
"Seed on the side of the hill"

From Long Valley *Ka wis ke on ca*, marking *Kauisik* boundaries, went "to the high peak where the sun sets, he called it *Mow it check mow win it* . . ." (Patencio 1943:96).

Schwenn notes that this peak is possibly Cornell Peak located due west of Mount San Jacinto and above the headwall of Snow Creek. Cornell Peak is the highly visible cone-shaped peak that stands on the ridge to the left of San Jacinto as seen from the Palm Springs area. However, from downtown Palm Springs near the Spa Hotel the high peak described may be near Hidden Lake divide or the rock mass on the south side of Tahquitz Creek at Caramba Camp.

Mukunpat (124)

Gifford says *Mukunpat* was the name of a clan of the Wildcat Moiety that lived with the *Morongo* and *Mohiyanim* clans, originally in Bear Valley, but also at *Yamisevul* in the Mission Creek area, *Maringa* and *Türka* (1918:180). Benedict says that *Mukunpat* was a place name for the *Mühiatnim* territory (1924:368). The location of the site is approximate.

The move to Mission Creek probably occurred shortly after the *Wanakik* had left the site.

Mum yum muck ca (125)

Ca wis ke on ca, marking boundaries, came down the ridge from a cold spring where they threw the horns of their game into a tall pine tree, to "the last water until reaching Tahquitz" (Patencio 1943:96).

Schwenn identifies this as the drainage at or near Laws Camp, or possibly Willow Creek.

Murray Hills Trail (126)

Possibly the present-day Thelman, Wildhorse, Hahn-Buena and Art Smith trails.

This trail went from the "Garden of Eden" back of Palm Springs past Eagle Spring, Magenesia Canyon, Cathedral Canyon, and on into the Deep Canyon area to join other trails (Patencio 1943:71).

Na che wit (127)   Algodones Dunes ?
"A country with nothing but sand"

After the death of *Mukat*, the smart and intelligent man *Pal mech cho wit*, "water not believing," "kept going toward the East. . . . He was seeing the mirage across the sand. He kept going on till he came to the sand country, sand and sand hills, which in the Indian language is called *na che wit* . . ." (Patencio 1943:24).

There are several dune fields in the Salton Trough, including the sand hills along the western side of the Coachella Valley and the North and South Algodones Dunes near Glamis. The sand hills are located north of Highway 111 and the Whitewater River wash and south of Indian Avenue, through portions of the Cities of Palm Desert, Indian Wells Bermuda Dunes, and north La Quinta. William Blake (1857) noted that the sand hills continued along the north side of the trail from Palm Springs to Travertine Point for about 3 or 4 miles east of Indian Wells (today the north end of the City of La Quinta, south of Washington Street).

Because of the reference to the mirage, the sand country referred to may be the North and South Algodones Dunes. The Algodones Dunes are located east of the Salton Sea, north of the town of Glamis. See also Sand Hills.

Na hal log wen et (128)   Snow Creek
"The center of an open space"

Evon ga net, establishing the boundaries of *Kauisik* territory, ". . . crossed Snow Creek, which he called *Na hal log wen et*, the center of an open place. At this place he took a rest. He lifted up his head and straightened his body" (Patencio 1943:54).

The mouth of Snow Creek was occupied by the *Teshana Wanakik* (Bean 1960).

Naialwawaka (129)

A place near Martinez to which Eagle Flower, *Aswitseī*, and his family (*Sēwahilem* lineage, Coyote moiety) moved after leaving *Tūva*" (Patencio 1943:43; Strong 1929:87, 42, 52).

Natcūta (130)

This village was located about one-half mile east of Horse Canyon and several miles northwest of the two villages at Old Santa Rosa, ie, northwest of Rockhouse Canyon. According to Strong's map (1929:145), the probable location is the "valley or flat" north of the Turkey Track and about one mile up Horse Canyon. Here a smaller tributary canyon, called White Wash, joins Horse Canyon.

This was the clan home of the *Natcūtakiktum lineage*, Coyote moiety. They were inactive by the 1920s (Strong 1929:146, 148). This group moved to San Timoteo Canyon in the nineteenth century (Strong 1929:91), but its members probably returned to Cahuilla Valley in the 1860s or 1870s.

Nauhañavitcem Village (131)

Mangalar Spring, at the south end of the Fig Tree Valley, is possibly the site of the *Nauhanavitcem* village which was an extension of *Wilīya*, the clan home.

Nauhañavitcem was the home of the *Nauhañavitcem* lineage, "people living in the center," Coyote moiety. This group was a subdivision of the *Wiwaiīstam* clan (Strong 1929:146, 148).

Nauhañavitcem may take its name from *nakwet*, the Cahuilla name for the Sugarbush, *Rhus ovata*, a species related to sumac. "The sumacs by the spring . . . are not tall but very old, gnarled, crabbed and heavily trunked. Mangalar Flats, which slopes gently down from the spring toward Coyote Creek, is covered with creosote bush, Mohave yucca, buckhorn cactus, catclaw, cheesebush and burroweed. On the hillsides above the spring are found desert apricot, sumac and beavertail (Schad 1986:171-172).

Ng natches pie ah (132)
"Spreading sand"

A place at the entrance of *Tachevah* (Dry Falls) Canyon back of Palm Springs, where there is fine white sand, highly prized by medicine men in their work, named by *Ca wis ke on ca* in going around *Kauisik* territory (Patencio 1943:98). This site is at the end of Alejo Road.

Nicholias (Nicolas) Canyon, Spring, and Village (133)

Nicholas Canyon opens into Rockhouse Valley. It is named after Nicolas Guanche, the last member of the Guanche family to live there.

Ninkicmu (Lin Kish mo) (134)

A rock named after one of the great *net's* three dogs: "Between these points occur three large rocks which he named for his three dogs, the first *awelmū*, the second *niñkicmū*, and the third *paklic*" (Strong 1929:101).

The points between which they lie are: *Malal*, the north point of Chino Canyon; *Pe on bel* (or *Pionvil*), the point between *Malal* and the south point of Blaisdell Canyon; *Ta was ah mo* (or *Teuamul*), the south point of Blaisdell Canyon; and *Ta mare* (or *Tama*), Windy Point (1929:101).

Num na sh b al (135)
A place of resting"

A rock located at the south point of Chino Canyon near Leaning Rock, about three feet high, smooth like a table on top, against which people rested when going along the old Indian trail up Chino Canyon. It was visited by *Ca Wis Ke On Ka* while going around *Kauisik* territory (Patencio 1943:98).

One Palm Creek (136)

This spring with one palm is near the mouth of Deep Canyon. Even though there is but the one palm, this is likely to have been a spot where hunters and travellers camped (Henderson 1961).

Ow kee ve lem (137)
"The place of the horns"

A place named by *Ca wis ke on ca*: "the place of the very cold spring, the water so cold it hurts the teeth. . . The hunters came to drink the water of this cold spring, and there they threw the horns of their game into a tall pine tree, till it hung full of them" (Patencio 1943:96).

Schwenn notes that there are two springs between Tahquitz Rock (Lily Rock) and Hidden Lake. The first, called Candy's Creek, is located along the trail from Tahquitz Valley to Laws Camp, just above Reed Meadow. The second spring is located along the trail between Saddle Junction (Skunk Cabbage Meadow) and Wellman's Divide and San Jacinto Peak at Wellman's Cienaga. *Ca wis ke on ca* had traveled from the "table top of pine trees" (Skunk Cabbage Meadow) to the north side of Hidden Lake (Long Valley) to the peak where the sun sets (Cornell Peak). He was probably returning in the same general direction from Round Valley to Wellman's Divide to the Cienaga to Caramba. This makes the spring at Wellman Cienaga the most likely possibility.

Pa cale (138)
"A water tank"

Ca wis ke on ca "went a short way north till he came to a gorge which is a huge crack in the mountain. Mrs. Austin McManus has built a Spanish home just beside it. In time of wet winters great flood waters pour through there. *Ca wis ke on ca* named this place *Pa cale*, a water tank. Somewhere in this great split rock is a water tank which has pure sweet water in the summer time. The Indian women lowered their water jars and filled them with water. This water was always to be had when the water of Tahquitz dried up" (Patencio 1943:97-98).

Mrs. McManus had two homes--one a pink Mediterranean-style house and the other, an adobe. The pink house was on the ledge behind or by the Palm Springs Tennis Club on Tahquitz Drive between the ends of Arenas and Barristo Avenue. The adobe, now the Historical Society Headquarters on South Palm Canyon, was once situated on the old Oasis Hotel site at Tahquitz and Palm Canyon.

There are several tinajas in the small canyon at the end of Barristo Road at Tahquitz Drive to the left of the main building of the Palm Springs Tennis Club.

Pa hal ke on a (139)   Sand Hills

"*Ca wis ke on ca* went across the valley to the sand hills. He called the sand hills *Pa hal ke on a*" (Patencio 1943:99).

The Indio Hills, particularly Edom Hill, are known as the sand hills. The sand hills extend from south of Indian Avenue to Indio paralleling Hwy 111 and Whitewater River channel.

Pah-wah'-te (140)   Magnesia Springs Canyon
"The drinker"

The main Murray Hill trail mentioned by Patencio (1943:71) crosses the mouth of this canyon. The source of water in the canyon was Magnesia Spring. Today the Canyon supports over a thousand *Washingtonia filifera* that grow in small groups along its length. There are several hundred-foot plus high water falls in the canyon.

Paint Island (141)

One of three islands (along with Pelican Island, Mullet Island and Three Buttes) in the Salton Sea that once were mud volcanoes. "Paint Island and Mullet Island are connected by paths. These paths are shoveled mud raised above the water level. They are dry on top, but shake like jelly underneath. . . . The wet paths that once rocked when you walked on them are dry and firm now. Now, where once springs were bubbling everywhere on Paint Island, it is a hard crust of salt" (Patencio 1971:17-18).

Paklic (142)

One of three rocks named by the great *net* for his three dogs (Strong 1929:101).

That named for *Paklic*, the third dog, should be located between the south point of Blaisdell Canyon and Windy Point.

Dogs sometimes served religious persons as familiars.

Palaiyil (143)
"Water turtle"

This village, the home of the *Panuksēkiktum*, Wildcat moiety, was located, according to Strong, about three miles northeast of Thermal on the east side of the Southern Pacific Railroad line. The *Panuksēkiktum* were subordinate to the *Kauwicpamēauitcem*, of which Cabezon was the chief (Strong 1929:41, 55; Gifford 1918:190).

This village would have stood about 80 to 100 feet above sea level which would have placed it 40 or more feet above the high stand of ancient Lake Cahuilla.

Palhanikalet (144)   Tahquitz Falls
"Water falling down" (Strong 1929:101)

Many members of the present-day Agua Caliente Band of Cahuilla Indians remember going up Tahquitz Canyon to swim in Tahquitz Creek beneath the falls. The falls have been a famous tourist attraction, even though they can be reached only on foot or on horseback.

Palhilikwinut (145)

A place near the head of Murray Canyon named by the great *net* (Strong 1929:100).

Pal hiliwit (146)
"Wide water"

Palhiliwit was a village about two miles south of where the Martinez Reservation buildings are now. It had a spring which provided sufficient water for some irrigation and for swimming in hot weather. It was the home of three clans: the *Mūmlētcem*, who owned the spring and are remembered as having eight houses; the *Masūwitcem*, who had seven houses; and the *Wiitem*, who had five houses. Each clan had its own *net* and dance house. All belonged to the Coyote moiety. The area to the west would have been used by these clans for hunting, gathering, and ceremonial activities (Strong 1929:42,51).

Paliliem hemki (147)
"Bat's house"

The original home, exact location unknown, in the Santa Rosa mountains for the

Tamulañitcem, meaning "knees bent together," who later moved to *Palpunivikiktum hemkī* near Alamo (Strong 1929:41).

Palm Canyon Trail (148)

Palm Canyon Trail extends some 15 miles from the mouth of Palm Canyon near Hermit's Bench to its present-day junction with Highway 74 near Ribbonwood. Numerous canyons and trails branch off along the length of the trail. Several springs, one at Agua Bonita, and mesquite, cottonwood and willow thickets are encountered along the trail. The trail originally ended at Vandeventer Flat and was known in the 1920s as Vandeventer Trail.

Palm Canyon Trail Shrines (149)

There are piles of pebbles or small rocks beside the trail up Palm Canyon (Henderson 1941).

Palms to Pines Trail (150)

This trail from the Palm Desert area up Carrizo Creek Canyon to Pinyon Crest on the edge of Pinyon Flat and then east to Deep Canyon, was an extremely important trail. It was used by desert peoples going into the mountains for pinyon harvesting, other gathering, hunting, and ceremonial events. The modern Palms to Pines highway follows it for some way from Palm Desert, but is less direct in the mountain area. The Gordon Trail was called the Palm to Pines Trail by Francisco Patencio.

Palmulūkalet (151)

The home of the *Wēwonicyauam* lineage, Coyote moiety, a group that was reported to be extinct by the 1920s (Strong 1929:42,54).

No definite location is given for this village except that it was very near *Tūīkiktumhemki* and northeast of Mecca. The latter village was located, according to Strong, half-way between Mecca and Thermal. This suggests possible locations for both villages on the Cabezon Reservation, Section 6, T6S, R8E, or to the east of *Tūīkiktumhemki*. In any case the village would have been west of the mouth of Painted Canyon where the village of *Maswut Helaanut* stood (Strong 1929:42, 54).

This village stood some 80 to 180 feet below sea level, depending on where the village actually stood, and this would place it some 120 to 220 feet below the high stand of ancient Lake Cahuilla.

Palo Verde Canyon (152)

An ancient trail connects this canyon to the Natural Rock Tanks in Smoke Tree Canyon where a one inch high olla was found. This area was and is frequented by mountain sheep (Reed 1963). The trail then continues north and west past Pyramid Peak to Wonderstone Wash and Rainbow Rock, where there are lithic scatters. A branch goes from the head of Wonderstone Canyon goes to Travertine Palms (see Wonderstone Trail). There area numerous agave plants along the trail.

Palo Verde Spring provides an important water supply at the head of Palo Verde Canyon (Reed 1963:116-117).

Palpīsa (153)

The clan home of the *Temewhanitcem*, Wildcat moiety (Strong 1929:147,148).

This village was probably located on Tripp Flats west of the now closed Baptista post office. Strong states that it was about six miles north of *Pauī* (Cahuilla) along the southern base of Thomas Mountain and his map (1929:145) shows that it was west of Bautista.

A trail heads east from Tripp Flats to the north end of the Ramona Reservation near Hog Lake.

Pal pis o wit (154)   Falls Springs ?
"Sour water"

Ca wis ke on ca, in the course of naming places within *Kauisik* territory, gave this name to a spring "of the high canyon, on the south of Tahquitz Canyon" even though the spring had good water rather than sour (Patencio 1943:97).

Schwenn notes that this is possibly an unnamed and unmapped spring near the head of the South Fork of Tahquitz Canyon and the top of the ridge forming the south wall of the canyon. In Tahquitz Canyon below, the South Fork joins the main fork of Tahquitz Canyon and Hidden Springs fork.

Palpūniviktum hemkī (155)
"Circle over water, living at"

Palpūniviktum hemkī was a village two miles east of Alamo (which was south of 74th Avenue on Pierce Street). It was the home of the *Palpunivikiktum* clan, and two lineages apparently subordinate to that clan: the *Tēviñakikyum* and the *Tamulañitcum*. These groups were respectively from *Ataki*, *Tevi* and *Paliliem hemkī* in the Santa Rosa Mountains. Each group in general had different gathering areas in the mountains, but they shared an area due west of Alamo, called *Ēova*, for gathering cactus in the spring and summer. Barrows recorded the names *Lawilvan* ("cottonwood") and *Sivel* ("sycamore") for this village, according to Strong, but Barrows says that these names were given to the site of Alamo (1900:34). Strong's informants did not recognize these names. Strong also says that *Palsīkal*, "water hole," was an old name for *Palpūniviktum hemki* (1929:41,50).

Palsētahut (Palseta) (156)
"Salt water"

A village at a place now just across the railroad tracks, east of the town of Coachella. It was occupied by the *Akawenekiktum* lineage, meaning "people living at the long ridge of mountains east of Indio" and a branch group, the *Taukatim lineage*. Both belonged to the Coyote moiety. The *Taukatim* later moved to *Palsētamul*, which was nearby (Strong 1929:42,55-56; Gifford 1918:191).

At 71 feet below sea level this village would have been some 111 feet below the high stand of ancient Lake Cahuilla (+40 feet).

The site of *Palsētahut* is now part of Cabezon Indian Reservation, which is located on parts of Sections 19, 30 & 32, T5S, R7E, SBBM, north of Highway 111 between Indio and Coachella plus Section 6, T6S, R8E, SBBM N of Highway 111 and NW of Mecca. Until 1901, the southern portion of the valley was known, by a variety of spellings, as Cabezon after Old, Old Chief Cabezon ("big-headed") whose Cahuilla name was given to the reservation (Gunther 1984:81-83).

Palsētamul (Pal-so'nul [Curtis 1926:163]) (157)
"Salt water agave; water *so'nul* (a plant)"
(Strong 1929:42, 55-56)

A village whose site is on the present-day Cabezon Indian Reservation. It was the home of the *Taukatim* lineage, Coyote moiety, relatives of the *Akawenekiktum* lineage, with whom they originally lived at *Palsētahut* (q.v.) (Strong 1929:42, 55-56; Gifford 1918:191; Curtis 1926:163).

At about 70 feet below sea level, this village could not have been occupied with ancient Lake Cahuilla was at its high stand at 40 feet above sea level.

Pal tē-wat (158)

"Water" and "Pinyon pine" (Barrows 1900:33; Bright 1967:xxvi).

A village in the vicinity of Indio, at or near the Twelve Apostle Palms, which was the home of the *Wavaaīkiktum lineage*, Coyote moiety (Strong 1929:42, 56; Curtis 1926:164; Gifford 1918:191).

This village stood about 10 to 20 feet below sea level and about 50 to 60 feet below the high stand of ancient Lake Cahuilla (+40').

Paltūkwic kaīkaīawit (Palkausinakela) (159)

"Blue water," "Little water coming from a spring"

This location had a warm spring and sufficient water for domestic uses, but not for irrigation. It lay beside the Salton Sea, and the *Wanticiñakik-tamianawitcem* clan moved there from *Tūva*, two miles south, about 1880. This was the clan of Juan Razon, generally known as "Fig Tree John" (Strong 1929:49). Gifford (1918:191) had reported Fig Tree John's clan as the *Palkausinakela*. Strong says "this was given as the place name of the site where Fig Tree John lived later" (1929:49). It is not clear from Strong's text whether *Palkausinakela* also referred to *Paltūkwic Kaīkaīawit*.

According to Cahuilla elder Alice Lopez, Juan Razon began to raise figs after some white people gave him some plants. (Teamsters on the Bradshaw trail used to stop at his place to change horses, and buy bundles of hay.) Alice remembers that Juan's son Jack Razon and his wife brought figs to her family when she was young. At first the children were reluctant to eat something so strange.

Juan had two sons, Jake and Mike Razon.

Alice's family used to go to Juan Razon's to visit, and she remembers him telling stories about the water babies that cried in his spring, especially if someone were going to die. Once in a while they could be seen on top of the water. They had red skin, and no hair. When they saw someone coming, they rolled back into the water. Water babies were also heard at the hot springs at Palm Springs (Vane 1970, 1979).

Paluknavitcem (160)   Stubbe Canyon & Village

"People living at"

This canyon was part of the territory owned by the *Wanakik* Cahuilla clan. Many archaeological sites have been recorded within it. Benedict reports it as the home of the *Palukiktum* group, which she mistakenly thought to be Serrano, and gave the place name *Palukiki* (1924:368). Strong gave it the place name *Paluknavitcem* (1929:91). Bean's informant, Victoria Wierick, identified the group that lived there as the *Palukna Wanakik* lineages of the *Wanakik* sib, one of ten lineages of the sib that were active in the early 19th century. It is no longer ceremonially active.

Pa-nach-sa (Panūksī) (161)

This is a mountain camp or village on the north side of Toro Peak described by Barrows as "high up on the north side of Torres" (1900:27). The *Wakaikiktum*, "Night herons," lived first at *Tciuk* "back in the Santa Rosa Mountains, then at *panūksī* at the head of a canyon about seven miles south of Indio, and later came to *mauūlmiī*" (Strong 1929:52).

Toro Peak is one of two summits on Santa Rosa Mountain, the other being Santa Rosa Peak. Santa Rosa Mountain itself was called Torres Mountain by Barrows. Schwenn notes that this could be the village at Agua Alta Spring. On the other hand, a location at the head of Guadalupe Canyon would place this village on the north side of Santa Rosa Mountain. It could be on the west or east side of Deep Canyon, but such a location would not likely be described as south of Indio.

Panoquk (162)   Palm Bowl

A bowl above 2450' elevation in Sheep Canyon surrounded by distinct peaks, called '*Panoquk*' by the Cahuilla Indians and 'Palm Bowl' by early cattlemen and settlers (Lindsay and Lindsay 1984:101).

Panyik (See Andreas Canyon Village) (10)

Par-powl (163)   Mud Volcanoes
"Water bewitched"   Salton Sea
"It always was bad country about those hills or islands even when the water was there. There were acres of boiling mud springs all around. The water was very hot. . . . Sometimes the mud pots . . . lie like pools on the ground, many feet across. But always boiling steam, hissing and whirling. The Indian people do not go very near them. It is very dangerous and there is nothing to go to them for. The Indians called the place *Par-powl* . . . and stayed away" (Patencio 1971:18-19).

Pasīawha (164)

The clan home of the *Tepamokiktum* or *Iswitim* clan, Wildcat moiety.

According to Strong's map, this village was located about six miles northeast of *Pauī* (Cahuilla) at the southeastern end of Pine Meadow along the northeast base of Thomas Mountain (Strong 1929:145). The village was located about one-half mile northwest of *Pauata*, the latter village located near the mouth of Penrod Canyon, southern end of Pine Meadow, east of and on the other side of Thomas Mountain from Bautista post office. Penrod Canyon was originally called Bull Canyon but that name has since been applied to the next canyon to the east.

The *Tepamōkiktum* and the *Hōkwitcakiktum* people were apparently lineages of the same clan, both being nicknamed "*iswitim*," meaning "wolf," said to have been given them because of a habit of eating meat (Strong 1929:147,148, 153; Kroeber 1908:35). "Lubo," Spanish for "wolf" is a family name at Cahuilla Reservation to the present day. See Pauata entry.

Paskwa (3)   Agua Bonita Spring ?
                                                                             Little Paradise Spring ?
A hot spring named by the great *net*: " a flat rock with mortar holes, at mouth of Palm Canyon, and halfway up the canyon *paskwa* a hot spring (rock mortars here also)" (Strong 1929:100).

Schwenn notes that there are several springs in the Canyon, the first just past the West Fork trailhead about 0.1 miles south of Hermit's Bench. This is a warm spring with group of palms surrounding it, one of which has "Hortensia" carved on its trunk. The next 2 springs about half way up canyon (south) from the mouth are Agua Bonita Spring and the spring at Little Paradise. Little Paradise has a single palm, and may not be a hot spring.

Pat-cha-wal (166)   San Ignacio

The most southerly village occupied exclusively by Cahuillas. The vicinity was originally used as a food gathering area by the *Wīwaiīstam* of Los Coyotes, who moved there to live after a smallpox epidemic struck them, necessitating the burning of their villages at Los Coyotes. To the south, their neighbors were the *Wilakal* people at San Ysidro, who were mixed Cahuilla, Cupeño, and Kumeyaay. By the 1920s, only one or two families remained at *Pat-cha-wal* (Strong 1929:146, 148,151; Barrows 1900:34).

A Cattle Round-up at Los Coyotes Indian Reservation

Many of the Cahuillas have been cowboys. This calf was roped at San Ignacio early in this century.

Pa:tsh yara:'nka' Wanet (167)

Pa:tsh yara:'nka' Wanet, according to Hill (1973:217), was the Serrano name for the Whitewater River, a stream important as a source of water and for the flora and fauna that it supported.

Pauata (168)

The clan home of the *Pauatīauitcem* lineage, Wildcat moiety. The village was located one-half mile southeast of *Pasīawha*, a village located six miles north of *Pauī* (Cahuilla) at the base of Thomas Mountain. It was probably located east of Bautiste post office, along the northeastern base of Thomas Mountain at the eastern end of Pine Meadow, near the mouth of Penrod Canyon (Strong 1929:145,147).

The *Pauatīauitcem* was one of the lineages that united under the leadership of Juan Antonio in the mid-nineteenth century and moved in 1846 to the Lugo rancho and then to San Timoteo Canyon (Strong 1929:91,164).

Penrod Canyon was named Bull Canyon on the 1897-98 USGS topo of the area, but on later maps the name, Bull Canyon, has been applied to the next canyon to the east.

Pauī (169)   Cahuilla (Coahuila)

An important Cahuilla town said to have been settled about 1875. "No one clan seems to have owned the warm sulphur springs and adjoining territory, for when it was permanently settled the localized clan organization had largely broken down and its inhabitants represented survivors of several of the eastern Mountain clans." About three families were living there in the 1920s. *Pauī* is now part of the Cahuilla Indian Reservation (Strong 1929:146-147,152).

Paukī (170)

This village was located on Terwilliger Flats, southeast of *Pauī* (Cahuilla) at La Puerta. No one clan appears to have claimed the locality though representatives of at least two clans lived there until the last few decades" (Strong 1929:147).

Pa ute em (171)

Evon ga net, marking the boundaries of *Kauisik* territory, ". . . went on to what is now Cathedral Canyon. . . From there he crossed the desert to the north, calling at the ground squirrel's home *Pa ute em*" (Patencio 1943:53).

Evon ga net was traveling from Cathedral Canyon toward Edom Hill. Ground squirrel's home was probably in and around Whitewater Wash, about one-half mile north of Hwy 111.

Both California and round-tailed ground squirrels are found in the sand dunes-mesquite habitat. The mesquite thickets (*P. juliflora*) are "mostly scattered along the edges of the Whitewater River and between Indian Wells and the foothill spurs to the south." Round-tailed and antelope ground squirrels are both found in creosote-palo verde habitat which, according to Ryan, is on flood plain of Deep Canyon (Ryan 1968:22, 29).

"The round-tailed ground squirrel makes his home in the sands or loose soils of the bleak desert flats, where wind and heat and shimmering light make life quite unbearable for many of the other animals. Befitting his harsh environment, he is a plain-looking fellow with a cinnamon-drab body built on the proportions of a rather slender cylinder, five or six inches long, with an almost earless, round baldish-appearing head at one end and a rather long round tail at the other, as Dr. Spencer F. Baird once said, 'in everything but the long rounded tail he is a miniature of the prairie dog.' . . .The burrows of this rodent are neither deep nor extensive. Like the underground runways of the kangaroos rats, they often cave in as you walk over them. . . Small colonies of these squirrels are widely scattered over the low-lying sand deserts, but nowhere are the animals plentiful" (Jaeger 1961:118-119, 121).

Pelican Island (174)

An island in the Salton Sea that was once notable as a pelican hatchery. At nesting time there were so many pelicans in the air that the island was lost to view (Patencio 1943:85; 1971:17-18).

Other Salton Sea islands are Paint Island, Mullet Island, and Three Buttes.

Pe on bel (Pīonvil) (172)
"Cool wind blowing"

A pile of rocks north of Palm Springs created by *Evon ga net*: "Then along the Whitewater ditch about three quarters of a mile he came to a large pile of rocks . . . At the point here it was dry and hot, so *Evon ga net* threw some small rocks against the hill, which caused a cool wind to blow, that is the meaning of the name *Pe on bel* " (Patencio 1943:54).

"The first rocky point beyond this bridge he called *pionvil . . .*" This bridge was the "second bridge on [the] highway from Palm Springs to Whitewater . . ." (Strong 1929:101).

Pionvil (Pe on bel) is the next point north of *Malal*, the north point of Chino Canyon. It is the rocky point between the north point of Chino Canyon and the south point of Blaisdell Canyon.

Pe ya hot mor am mah (173)   Song Point
"The place of the army worms"

A place near the Araby tract named by *Evon ga net* (Patencio 1943:53). This is possibly the point along Hwy 111 just east of El Cielo and Palm Canyon wash where Southridge Dr meets the highway. Song Point is west of the small canyon to the west of Eagle Canyon and near or east of the Araby Tract.

Army worms, *Homoncocnemis fortis (Lepidoptera:Noctuidae)* are caterpillars "mostly hairless, some 30 to 50 mm. in length, of varying colors, usually striped or mottled, and are usually nocturnal [Essig 1958]. The army worms appear in great numbers, feeding on grasses, trees, and other vegetation (Sutton 1988:41).

Wright left this account of Cahuilla harvesting caterpillars: "vast armies of caterpillars . . . they are huge worms three and four inches long. [A] small army of Indians [men, women, and children] are out gathering them as though they were huckleberries, for use as food. Seizing a fat worm, they pull off its head, and by a dexterous jerk the viscera are ejected, and the wriggling carcass is put into a small basket or bat, or strung in strings upon the arm or about the neck, till occasion is found to put them into a large receptacle. At night, these Indians carry their prey home, where they have a great feast. Indians from a long distance came to these worm feasts, and it is a time of great rejoicing among them. The larvae that are not consumed at the time (and they eat incredible quantities), are put upon ground previously heated by a fire, and thoroughly dried, when they are packed away whole, or pulverized into a meal" (Wright 1884:238, cited by Sutton 1988:39).

Pierce Ranch and Springs (175)

This area figured in Willie Boy's flight (Lawton 1960). Willie Boy has the character now of a legendary figure among Cahuillas and Chemehuevis.

Pinalata (177)

A place north and west of *Simuta*, Indian Potrero, named by the great *net* in marking *Kauisik* boundaries (Strong 1929:100).

Pinyon Flat (178)

Pinyon Flat was a uniquely valuable place for food collecting and hunting game for the Cahuilla. The area was used by many groups, but apparently not owned by any particular group. Informants in the 1960s recalled to Bean that pinyon crops were available to whomever was able to get there first. People from many villages that lay at the mouths of Palm Canyon, San Andreas Canyon, Deep Canyon, Martinez Canyon, and Santa Rosa Canyon--all would come into the area when the pinyon nuts were ready for harvesting and camp there for a short time, and then leave.

Alice Lopez remembers that her mother used to tell of going along to harvest pinyon at Pinyon Flat when she was young, which would have been in the 1860s or 1870s. She rode horseback from Martinez, where she lived, up Martinez Canyon, accompanying her uncle. Before they picked any nuts they put food in the Big House for three days, and ceremonially--a first fruits rite. Alice's mother's task was to carry water for the nut pickers. Picking nuts was hard work. Someone had to climb trees and hit the pine cones with sticks to get them loose. They were put in sacks (they made the hands sticky) and carried home. Then a fire of brush was built in the sand, and the nuts were buried overnight in the hot sand pit. In the morning they were taken out and pounded on a rock to make the seeds come out. They stayed at the Flat for a week.

At Santa Rosa, Alice's mother's sister put food in the Big House for three days before going to Pinyon Flat (Vane field notes, 1979).

Pinyon Flat lay at a place where the boundaries of many clans' territories met. Its function as a "common area" had the effect of limiting conflict over a valuable food resource which was unstable. In contrast to acorn producing oaks and mesquite trees, the pinyons were erratic in their production from year to year while the former were stable. Given the stability of the acorn and mesquite bean supplies, the political energy necessary to maintain strict ownership rules with respect to pinyons was probably non-efficient for the Cahuilla. The enforcement of the rules would have led to conflict (Bean 1972:129; Bean and Saubel 1972:102-105).

See *Kwa-le-ki*.

Pisata (Piatopa) (176)   Banning Water Canyon Village

A village in what is now Banning Water Canyon that was the home of the *Pisatanavitcem* lineage, Coyote moiety, of the *Wanakik* Cahuilla. The Romero expedition reported a Spanish rancho as being there in 1823. The lineage was no longer active in the 1920s (Strong 1929:91; Bean and Mason 1962:35; Gifford 1918:191).

Place West Of Toro (179)

"From there he [*Aswitsei*, Eagle Flower] came south along the San Jacinto Mountains to a place west of Toro; he was weeping and he pushed a hole in the ground with his staff which is still there" (Strong 1929:86).

This place may be in La Quinta Cove.

Potrero Spring (180)

This spring lies on the trail between Palm Canyon and Pinyon Flat, and was an important source of water for people travelling from Palm Canyon to Pinyon Flat where they went to gather pinyon nuts each year and for other reasons such as hunting and gathering other food resources. Potrero Canyon, in which it lies, was formerly called Horse Potrero Canyon (q.v.).

Pow ool (Poo ool) (181)   Hidden Lake

The mountain lake that *Ca wis ke on ca* named after the "flat tule that grew in the middle of the lake." He also found the "very large mescal which grew on the lower side of Hidden Lake in very far places (Patencio 1943:86, 96). This lake was a sacred place, associated with the acquisition of supernatural power.

Fragments of the old Cahuilla Trail have been found at Hidden Lake. This is the hunting trail that is mentioned by Francisco Patencio and descends the ridge line west of Tahquitz Canyon down to Palm Springs. It is currently known as the Skyline, Sunrise, and Chino Trail. It now begins at the end of Ramon Road and ends near the Tram building.

Pūichekiva **(182)**
"Road Runner's House"

A village site within what is now Torres-Martinez Reservation. This was one of the most important Cahuilla villages in the desert from perhaps about 1850. It was the home of Strong's consultant, Francisco Nombres, and was used by Strong as an example of a "typical Desert Cahuilla village of fifty-odd years ago." The village broke up because of a water shortage when the water table fell about the turn
of the century (Strong 1929:45-49; Bean field notes).

Romero arrived at the villages in this area on January 18, 1823, and left this description: "At the above-mentioned hour we began to travel through the mezquitales and the rancherias that there are, until the sixth rancheria, where we arrived at 12:00 and finding a little zacate, we rested until 3:00 when we proceeded through mezquitales to the rinconada (narrow valley) where we arrived at 8:00 at night . . . This 'Rinconada' is located to the west, and to the east (are) several rancherias between the mezquitales and the sierra in both directions, which we knew because of the great amount of smoke which went up, and Indians who came out to look at us at several points, which we have noticed since our departure from Los Veranitos today" (Bean & Mason 1962:47-48).

"Martinez," the home of an Indian named Martinez was listed as a village on Bradshaw's list of places on his route to La Pax in the 1860s (Gunther 1984:312).

Bancroft, in his "Guide to the Colorado Mines" described a stop at Martinez: "The only water . . . is in a few small wells, most of them a quarter of a mile from the road, and soon exhausted. This is another Indian village, much scattered, but containing several adobe structures, makes a more pretentious appearance than the others. Corn and sometimes barley can be had there. The place is

Indian Well at Torres, 1903

"I ran across it at Torres, east of Palm Springs in 1903. The approach down the steps was 20 feet below the top and the water stood 50 feet below that. I was told by Capt. Torres that it was dug by his people, the Cahuillas about 75 years before" (Letter by C. C. Pierce, photographer, November 7, 1938).

embowered with mesquite trees, which grow with great luxuriance, the bean being gathered in large quantities by the names" (1933:9, cited by Gunther 1984:312).

Water was so close to the surface that distinctive walk-in wells were used as a source of water. One traveler in 1862 noted: "at Martinez . . . we had to procure water by a very tedious process. The Indians had wells some twelve or fifteen feet deep into which seeped a small quantity of water. Down into these we were compelled to go upon poles with notches cut [along them for steps. The water was dipped up, a cupful at a time, poured] into a bucket and carried to the surface. No more than three or four buckets could be obtained in an hour" (Fairchild 1933:13).

"George Wharton James visited Martinez in 1905 or thereabout. He talked to Poncho Lomas, captain of the village at that time, who said the Martinez Indians were originally called *'E-va-at*, which signified people. They came into the desert from over the San Jacinto Mountains, through originally, 'in the beginning,' as he put it, they came from the East. Those who settled into this spot found the surface water which led to the digging of the well, and there were many mesquite and other good things to eat that grew profusely. The mountains were close by where there was an abundance of game, so they settled here and were content. Then the waters rose on the desert and drove them forth, and they ascended Martinez Canyon, toward the village of Santa Rosa, and lived there for many years, catching fish from the inland sea" (James 1906:239, cited by Gunther 1984:313).

Pul lo cla (Poo on loo la, Pu loo cla, Pūlūkla) (183) Ansell Rock ?
"Top of the ridge"

A large rock near Tahquitz Peak, given much power by *Evon ga net*. "From there the thunder comes and the earthquakes, much sound. He did this for his people, that they should have good hunting" (Patencio 1943:52, 88, 87; Strong 1929:100).

It is also described as "a hill to which hunters would sing in the dance house in order to have deer sent to them" (Strong 1929:100).

Schwenn notes that this rock can't be Lily (Tahquitz) Rock (see below). If you stand on Tahquitz Peak when a storm is over San Jacinto, the thunder rolls down the Tahquitz Valley bouncing off the San Jacinto-Jean-Marion ridge and the Tahquitz-Grey Tahquitz-Red Tahquitz ridge. Marion has a large rock on its summit but it is southwest of San Jacinto.

The next prominent peak southeast of Tahquitz after rounded South Peak is notched-shaped Ansell Rock. Starting on the Desert Divide heading NNW toward San Jacinto are Palm View, Spitler, Apache, Ansell Rock, and South Peaks. From the Divide one can look down into Palm Canyon and should be able to see Seven Palms. Of these peaks only Ansell Rock is a large rock on top of the ridge and is visible from Palm Canyon, Palm Springs and much of the valley floor down to Palm Desert.

Pūllūvil (184) Rock Monolith at *Tachevah* (Dry Falls) Canyon

The large smooth rock cliff at *Tachevah*, Dry Falls, back of Palm Springs, which was named by the great *net* (Strong 1929:100).

Qua al hec ik (185) Hawk Canyon
"Home of the hawk"

Evon ga net, laying out a place for the *Kauisik*, "came to what is now known as the Araby Tract. This he called *Qua al hec ik*, the home of the hawk, or hawk canyon." (Patencio 1943:53).

"The last Pony Express rider who came through this country was killed by renegade Indians-- by two very bad men--Andreas of Seven Palms, and Venturo of Stubby Creek. These two attacked the rider as he was passing Hawk Canyon, now the Araby Tract. This canyon had always been called Hawk Canyon, ever since *Evon-ga-net* came through and named every place. But after the murder it was sometimes called Robber Canyon.

These two men killed the Pony Express rider and took his money, saddle and bridle, and all that he had. His body they left half buried in Hawk Canyon. . . . the murdered man was a young fellow who had a wife and three sons and lived in San Bernardino. . . . The White Men . . . went to Hawk Canyon and found the body of the Pony Express rider half buried. They took him away and buried him at Gilman's Station" (Patencio 1971:21-22).

Qua al hec is the otherwise unnamed canyon behind the Araby Tract. Araby Drive & Escoba have a common intersection with Hwy 111--the Araby Tract was to the south of the highway at the base of Smoke Tree Mountain. It consisted of 80 acres near the base of the mountains between Palm Springs and Cathedral City. It was platted in June, 1925 (Gunther 1984:28).

Quawish-Ulish (186)   Mecca Hills
"Red Hills"

"The Mecca Hills is a basalt material collection area" as well as an area of ritual significance (Knack 1980:48).

Queri kitch (187)   San Gorgonio Mountain/Peak
"Bald or smooth"

The early people who could fly, the *Moh Moh Pechem*, flew from Cucamonga Mountain, *Evo Quish*, to San Gorgonio Mountain, which they called *Queri Kitch* (Patencio 1943:33).

Rattlesnake Canyon (189)

The Rattlesnake Canyon in present-day Anza Borrego State Park was an important area for hunting, especially for mountain sheep, which frequented the rock tanks and springs in the area for water (Reed 1963). There are at least four other Rattlesnake Canyons in the region.

Rattlesnake Spring (189)

A permanent spring in the Santa Rosa Mountains, now in Anza-Borrego State Park. It was an important water source for hunters. Near it is the site of an Indian camp or village (Reed 1963:126).

Rock in Palm Canyon (190)

After the head man, was killed, the *Mo Moh Pechem* "did not fly, but walked down across the mountain side to Palm Canyon. Then the third head man of the tribe decided that he would not go any further. He turned himself into a rock, and he is there in the rock yet" (Patencio 1943:33).

Rock near Top Of San Jacinto (191)

"There is a place near the top which has no pine trees, a place of about forty or fifty acres; right in the center of this place is a large smooth rock, about ten or fifteen feet square, not very high from the ground, about three feet. There they [*Mo Moh Pechem* people] stayed for a long time.

"From here they saw a mountain lion coming, and they said that if you saw it once, you could not see it again. But the headman of the tribe said that he could see it again. . . . The headman went and stood on the top of the rock, looking . . . Then the lion leaped upon the rock before he saw the man, and they began to fight, and both died there" (Patencio 1943:33).

This spot has not been located, but it may be on or near Folly, Miller, Jean Peaks, or Round Valley; forty to fifty acres is about 1/4 mile square.

Rock Tanks (192)

Rock tanks lie near the head of Smoke Tree Canyon and at the end of a trail coming up Palo Verde Wash. They are likely to have been an important source of water to travellors and hunters in this part of the Anza-Borrego Desert.

There are also natural rock tanks (the "Sheep Tanks") at about 2000 feet elevation in the Santa Rosa Mountains in Palm Wash. Reed reports seeing five of them, and another up the mountain to the east. He says the old-timers called them sheep tanks because "of the Big Horn Sheep watering there after heavy rains when these holes in the boulders are filled with water as the water runs down the canyons that have such places in the bottoms" (1963:117). It must be assumed that these were important to Native American hunters not only for the water they held, but also for the wild life they attracted, especially the sheep. There is a picture of one of the tanks in Reed (1963:119).

Rockhouse Canyon (194) See *Ataki*.

See discussion in "Cahuilla Regions" chapter.

Rockhouse Canyon is mentioned in Seiler's version of the story of Yellowbody that begins with two brothers and their mother. The younger brother dies; so the older brother and his mother go to Rockhouse Canyon and live there for a time (Seiler 1970:64-65). In Patencio's version of the story, the story takes place in part on Santa Rosa Mountain, but not specifically in Rockhouse Canyon (Patencio 1943:37-40).

Rockhouse Valley Peppergrass Gathering Area (195)

An area in Rockhouse Valley where *pakil*, peppergrass (*Lepidium nitidum*), was gathered. It was used in an infusion "to wash hair, keep the scalp clean, and prevent baldness" (Bean and Saubel 1972:85).

San Felipe Valley (196)

From *Ulicpatciat* village near Travertine Point and Fish Springs, the *Mo Moh Pechem* people flew "to the San Felipe Valley, to another open place on the place, and here they stayed . . .and raised large families. Then an animal, *To quastto hut*, which means an animal that comes from the sky with much noise of thunder, he came and took two or three of these people every day" (Patencio 1943:34).

In the story of *Esel I Hut*, the location of the village to which *To Quastto Hut* comes is given as the end of the Santa Rosa Mountains, ie., the vicinity of Travertine Point. ". . . he [*Esel I Hut*] went on to the end of the Santa Rosa range, to the place of the *Mo moh pechem* people. There he found a large village of many houses, and he spent all of one day trying to find someone living there; but the whole place was wiped out by the *To quastto hut*, the sky animal that was eating two and three of the people every day" (Patencio 1943:35).

Santa Catarina Spring Village (197)

This village, last occupied about 4 generations ago, was located at Santa Catarina Spring and is the "largest Indian site in the northern half of the [Anza-Borrego] Park . . .. A heavy deposit of middens overlays a large area" (Lindsay and Lindsay 1984:91).

Note: Santa Catarina Spring, located on the west side of Lower Willows in Coyote Canyon, is one of the main sources of the canyon's permanent water supply.

Father Pedro Font estimated in the winter of 1775-76 that this village in Coyote Canyon had a population of about 40 individuals (Lindsay and Lindsay 1984:105). This is a very low estimate, typical of Font, upon whose approach the Cahuillas hid from view.

Santa Rosa Spring (198)

A spring on Virgin Spring trail west of Stump Spring.

Sauic (199)   Salvador Canyon Village
                                                           Formerly Thousand Palms Canyon

Clan home of the *Sauicpakiktum (Sow-wis-pah-kik-tem)*, a Coyote moiety lineage of the *Wiwaiistam clan*, who divided and moved sometime prior to the 1850s to *Sewia* (New Santa Rosa) and *Kewel* (Cottonwood Springs, Rockhouse Valley) (Strong 1929:146, 148, 151).

According to Strong's map (p. 145, 1929), this village was located near the mouth of Thousand Palm Canyon, a tributary of Coyote Canyon. Thousand Palms Canyon, now mapped as Salvador Canyon after Salvador Ygnacio Linares, youngest member of the Anza expedition who was born just to the west. It contains over 360 palms. See Salvador Canyon. (Randall Henderson, Desert Magazine; Lindsay and Lindsay 1984:92). Just to the south of Salvador Canyon is the confluence of Indian, Cougar and Sheep Canyons.

Sauïvil (200)

Clan home of the *Sauïvilem*, a lineage of the *Wiwaiistam* clan, Coyote moiety (Strong 1929:146, 148). No location is given except for Coyote Canyon. The group moved to Warner's Hot Springs, *Kupa*, prior to the 1850s, perhaps after the Garra revolt (Phillips 1975) was quelled. Because of better farming land and job opportunities, many moved to Morongo by the 1880s and 1890s.

Saupalpa (201)

Clan home of the *Apapatcem (Nalgāliem)* lineage, Wildcat moiety. This village was located about 3 miles northwest of *Paui* (Cahuilla) along the east-southeast base of Cahuilla Mountain. Strong's estimate of 6 miles is inaccurate as this would place the village on the other side of Cahuilla Mountain (Strong 1929:145, 147).

Sawit ha push (202)   Hidden Palms, Indio Hills
"Snake's eye"

When the descendants of *Ca wis ke on ca* at Palm Springs separated into lineages, the family of the third and youngest brother moved far away over to Thousand Palms Canyon . . . But he was still dissatisfied, and moved farther down the valley to a place called the Snake's Eye . . . There he lived and raised a large family" (Patencio 1943:90).

This lineage may have moved to the small canyon between Pushawalla & Thousand Palms Canyon where Hidden and Horseshoe Palms oases are located. This canyon was in the past the outlet of Pushawalla Canyon before the San Andreas Fault moved the outlet or the lower end of the canyon westward.

Sec he (203)   Palm Springs
"The sound of boiling water"   Agua Caliente

One of the places where the *Kauisiktum* lineage, Wildcat moiety, lived.

"The head man, *Tu to meet*, was tired and sick and lame, so he took his *who' ya no hut* (staff of power), which he struck in the ground. He twisted it around, and caused the water of a spring come out--now Palm Springs Hot Spring. He named it *Sec he*, meaning boiling water, which is up to the earth and on the earth, which is to be for ever, never to dry up, never to go away, but to be there for ever and always for the sick" (Patencio 1943:100).

"This spring never had palms around it. The palms were brought and planted there by the people. The tules grew and the mesquite was thick. The thicket of mesquite run to the south of the spring, several blocks. The spring was choked with it" (Patencio 1943:94).

". . .the Pony Express ran through Palm Springs. I was too small to remember it, but all the Indians of that time, they remember all about it. . . . The route the riders took was from Yuma to Chuckawalla Valley. From there to Dos Palmas, across the valley to the Martinez Indians, on to El Torro and then to Indian Wells. From there they came to Agua Caliente (Palm Springs) and to Whitewater Point. Then they went on to Gilman's Station (Banning) and to San Bernardino. From there they went on to Los Angeles and San Francisco" (Patencio 1971:21).

"After the Pony Express did not run any more, the stages began coming through. . . . Jack Summers was agent at Palm Springs. He was the first white man to live here. He rented from ten to twelve acres where the Desert Inn now stands, and hired the Indians to raise barley for his horses. He also rented about the same amount just south of where the new school-house is built. He paid the Indians who worked the land for him, a team of horses, a set of harness, a plow, and some money for the year's work. But that year the water was low, and it turned out no good. . . . so they hired the Indians to go and gather galleta grass . . . and paid for it by weight. . . . Summers and his wife lived in an Adobe Station. It was made of sticks and brush plastered with adobe mud. This adobe was bought from the Indians. It came from the Spring. . . . This station was where the Post Office now stands" (Patencio 1943:60-61).

The hot springs at Palm Springs were not only the principal focus of *Kauisik* territory, but also the principal attraction for the non-Indians who have helped make Palm Springs a world class resort. Most of the Agua Caliene Band of Cahuilla Indians made their homes until recent years on Section 14, Township 4 South, Range 4 East, S.B.M., upon which it lies. The hot springs are now a feature of the Palm Springs Spa Hotel, which is owned by the band as a whole.

Sēūpa (204)

A village in a small valley on the Cahuilla Indian Reservation, about three miles southeast of *Pauī*. There is a spring there surrounded by willows and cottonwoods, and several fields of alfalfa and grain in the 1920s. It was the home of the *Natcūtakiktum* Clan, family name Arenas, who had moved there from their clan village of *Natcūta*, where they had previously lived. This village was about three miles southeast of *Pauī*. Strong was able to formulate the structure of the clan about 1860 when there were eight male clan members. One of these was Lee Arenas, later an important member of the Agua Caliente Band in Palm Springs (Strong 1929:147, 156).

Sewakil (205)

Sewakil is given by Gifford both as the name of a lineage and of the place south of Indio where the lineage lived. This was the lineage of Maria Augustine, who came from the Augustine Indian Reservation, where the *Sewakil* must have lived (Gifford 1918:191).

Sēwiū (San we yet) (Sewi) (Sēwīa) (Sewiat) (206)   (New) Santa Rosa

A village, whose name is variously spelled, on the south slope of Santa Rosa Mountain, sometimes located on what later was the Vandeventer Ranch and is now part of Santa Rosa Reservation. The *Sauicpakiktum* lineage moved there from Thousand Palms Canyon off Collins

Valley in the late 19th century (Barrows 1900:37; Kroeber 1925:694; James 1918; Strong 1929:145-146, 151).

A very important place if Gifford is correct in identifying it as the place where the Cahuilla gods, *Mukat* and *Temaiyowit*, died, and where the first people turned to rock:

"The coyote clans are said to have come from the region of Riverside (also to the northwest), proceeding first to *Sewiat*, a (mythical) locality in the San Jacinto Mountains. At *Sewiat* there is a cave with writing (pictographs?), also a 'big rock house.' This is beyond the house of the . . . spirit *Takwitc* on San Jacinto Mountain. The people who lived in ancient times have turned to rock at *Sewiat*. The gods died there (Gifford 1918:189).

Taxtemyauwitcem, a coyote man, lived at *Sewiat*. *Taxotesinigic* sent his sister to marry him" (Gifford 1918:189). [Gifford's parenthetical comments.]

"Another head man named *Mul li kik* settled at Van De Venter on the Santa Rosa Mountain and called at that time *San we yet*. Many of the people settled there" (Patencio 1943:37).

According to Merriam, the original name of the village at Vandeventer Flat was *Sowis-is-pakh* (Merriam field notes). The name was probably taken from the name of the *Sauicpakiktum*, a Cahuilla lineage that was originally from the Los Coyotes area. See **Sauic**.

Sewi is noted as marking the southwestern boundary of the territory of the *Kauisiktum* clan. It was named by the "great *net*" and lies at the south end of Palm Canyon (Strong 1929:100). It was probably near to or the same as *Se'-o-ye* (Smith 1909) at Vandeventer Flat or *Sēwia* (Strong 1929:145-157).

Sēwitckul (207)   Murray Hill

The hill east of the mouth of Andreas Canyon named by the great *net* (Strong 1929:100).

The mountain sheep went to the top of it at lambing time: "Here it is warm and sunny on the slopes of this high hill. The rams keep a lookout for danger all about the whole country (Patencio 1943:16,71).

Sheep Canyon and Alamo Canyons (208)

These canyons in the Santa Rosa Mountains west of the Salton Sea, whose names are interchanged from one topo edition to another, comprised a hunting and gathering area for the people who lived in Agua Dulce and *Iviatim*. This whole area was frequented by mountain sheep. There is another Sheep Canyon that is a tributary to Coyote Canyon on the south flank of the Santa Rosa Mountains.

Sherman Shady Spring (209)

This spring was a water source for the *Maringa* clan of Serranos.

Sim mo ta (Simuta) (Tev koo hul ya me) (210)   Indian Potrero, Palm Canyon

The Cahuilla culture hero, *Evon ga net* "came down near to what is now called Palm Canyon. He called this country *Sim mo ta*, meaning Indian corral or pasture" (Patencio 1943:53).

The great *net* named *Simūta* as he marked out *Kauisik* territory: ". . . more rock mortar holes, about 5 miles west of Palm Canyon" (Strong 1929:100).

According to Hooper, this was once a village site occupied by a group called the *Simotakiktem*, all of whose people were killed: "Long ago, there was a clan or village called *Simotakiktem* about six miles south of Agua Caliente. There was one man in the clan who caused a great deal of trouble for the surrounding groups. So these got together and decided to make war on the entire group. When the *Simotakiktem* saw the other Cahuilla coming, they hid in a big round rock which was just like a room and had a stone door. The Cahuilla surrounded them, forced the door, and threw firebrands inside, then closed the door. They were all suffocated (Hooper 1920:355-356).

After the war with the Seven Palms people, the "older men carried the heads [of the Seven Palms chiefs and headmen] to Palm Canyon, to a place now called Indian Potrero, above the mesquite trees" (Patencio 1943:89). See *You koo hul ya me*.

Indian Potrero is about five miles south of the mouth of Andreas Canyon. There are several bedrock mortars and a large palm oasis on the potrero. Cedar Creek, which issues from the spring of that name high on the Desert Divide, flows through the oasis. Agave roasting pits can be found in nearby Palm Canyon and Bullseye Rock is south down Cedar Creek from Indian Potrero.

Smoke Tree Canyon (211)

A canyon in the eastern Santa Rosa Mountains. It is marked by the presence of natural rock tanks which provided a source of water for mountain sheep and wild life as well as Indians while in the area. The sides of the canyons show many trails, apparently made by sheep (Reed 1963).

So-kut Men-yil (212)
"Deer" "moon"

This name was given to an irrigated area in the village of *Pūichekiva*, home of the *Wantcauem*, Coyote moiety. Barrows was told that it was once a famous village "in which to hunt the deer in the moonlight" (1900:33). Strong identified it as a spot at *Puichekiva* where there was surface water (1929:44, Ftnt. 52).

Pūichekiva was about a mile north of the present reservation buildings at Martinez Indian Reseervation.

Stump Spring (213)

A spring on a small trail that branches off the Virgin Spring trail west of Cedar Spring. This small trail goes north and west, ending at Stump Spring.

Sum mat chee ah wen e (214)
"Bunched hay"

A peak named by *Ca wis ke on ca* naming points on the boundary of *Kauisik* territory: "From there the trail separated, one going down what is now the Gordon (Palm and Pines) trail, and the other coming down the ridge of the Tahquitz Canyon. He stopped at the spring of the high canyon, on the south of Tahquitz Canyon. . . . He went up to the first dark peak, where the sun sets, and he called that peak *Sum mat chee ah wen e* . . ." (Patencio 1943:97).

This is the high bump on the south ridge of Tahquitz Canyon above the junction of Tahquitz with the Hidden Fork and the South Fork. From this point the trail into Tahquitz probably descended precipitously down the south wall to cross the creek in the vicinity of the junction of Tahquitz Creek with the unnamed west and northwest forks. The northwest fork is known locally as Rattlesnake Canyon and this location is above the fourth falls. The trail may have followed the canyon for a short distance but then climbed out of the canyon on the north side to high point, elevation 5705'. At this point the trail joins the present-day Skyline Trail. At high point 5705 on the Skyline Trail is a trail junction with a trail descending into Tahquitz Canyon, destination Falls Spring. The sign reads: "Falls Springs, 5 hours." The present-day Skyline Trail follows the old Cahuilla hunting trail to Hidden Lake (Patencio 1943:70-71).

Sung pa (215)   Cedar Spring and Palm View Peak
"Coarse porous rock"
  Evon ga net, hunting for more places for his people, went from Idyllwild and a spring near there (probably Apache Spring) "until he came to a mountain and a spring, about half a mile from the main ridge, he named this mountain and spring *Sung pa . . .*" (Patencio 1943:53).
  Schwenn notes that there are two springs about one-half mile from the Desert Divide (ridge running from Tahquitz Peak and Lookout Mountain (now the route of Highway 74). These are Apache Spring on the east slope of Apache Peak, and Cedar Spring on the east slope of Palm View Peak. (See Apache Spring, *Cow quish hec i.*) Cedar Spring takes its name from the Incense Cedars growing at the spring. In addition black oaks, canyon live oaks and service berry grow along the trail from the main ridge to Cedar Spring. The 1959 USGS Idyllwild 15-min topo shows a trail along the east side of the Desert Divide from Apache Spring to Fobes Saddle, between Apache and Spitler Peaks, along the ridge to the summit of Palm View Peak and then southeast along the ridge. Two trails drop from the Desert Divide to Cedar Spring, one from Palm View Peak to Lion Spring and then to Cedar Spring and the other from the saddle west of Little Desert Peak northward and down to Cedar Spring. The latter trail is a continuation of the Cedar Springs Trail which climbs up the west side of the ridge from Tripp Meadow and Morris Ranch Road. This trail continues past Cedar Spring to Little Camp Spring and then Agua Fuerte Spring and then down the West Fork of Palm Canyon to the Needles Eye and Hermit's bench in Palm Canyon. There are said to be petroglyphs at the Camp Scherman Girl Scout camp located near the trailhead on Morris Ranch Road. See *Tep po we.*

Ta che va (184)   Tachevah Falls Canyon
"A plain view"   Dry Falls Canyon
  Ca wis ke on ca, tracing *Kauisik* boundaries, "went to what is now Dry Falls. He called that place *Ta che va . . .*" (Patencio 1943:98).
  See also *Ng natches pie ah*, *Tachevah* Canyon Entrance, and *Pulluvil*, *Tachevah* Canyon Rock Monolith.
  Ta che va is the large slab of rock, a rock monolith, that stands out prominently on the mountain wall rising in back of Palm Springs. Several hundred feet high, it stands on a cliff west of the mouth of *Tachevah* Canyon.

Tachi-maulum (216)
From "*maulum*," meaning "palms"
  A place east of Indio, between Indio and the Mecca Hills. According to Curtis it was "northeast of Indio" and was "a favorite place for harvesting mesquite beans, which are here very sweet, and for gathering basketry material and palm fruit" (Curtis 1926:164).
  Curtis' directions are off by 45 degrees; hence, this would be east of Indio, possibly between the Whitewater River channel and the base of the Mecca Hills. This area is below sea level and therefore below the high water line of the last stand of Lake Cahuilla. The mesquite in this area is predominantly screw-bean mesquite.

Tahquish heki (217)   The San Jacinto Mountains
"The home of *Tahquish*"
  Tahquitz Peak is thought of as the home of one of the supernatural beings from creation time, *Tahquish*, about whom much Cahuilla (and other southern California Indian) oral literature is centered. A common story line tells of *Tahquish* stealing a young woman and taking her into the mountain. She is allowed to return to her people, but is adjured not to tell where she had been. When she breaks down and tells, she disappears forever. *Tahquish* commonly manifests himself in thunderbolts and lightening. As a guardian spirit to shamans, he served as a source of great power.
  The name *Tahquish heki*, which Katherine Saubel gives as the name of not just the peak, but of the entire San Jacinto range, indicates that *Tahquish* for the Cahuilla lived not only in Tahquitz

Peak, but in the range as a whole. (See Bean and Vane's forthcoming report on the Tahquitz Canyon Project, 1991).

Tahquitz Canyon (86)

See *Kakwawit*.

Tahquitz Creek (26)

"The country long ago was not like it is now. . . . Tahquitz was a good stream always -- winter and summer. . . .But one time (I was very small, I could not remember yet), there came such earthquakes as had not been known to any of the people. . . . Then it was that Tahquitz Creek went dry, and only ran water in the winter time . . ." (Patencio 1943:58).

This passage probably refers to the January 9, 1857 Fort Tejon Earthquake, San Andreas Fault, estimated magnitude--8.0, and epicenter--Fort Tejon, California, Intensity at Fort Tejon-- about VII+ & Coachella Valley--about VI+. Charles Richter reports: "For 1857 our reports come mostly from untrained observers; the area over which shaking was felt, in spite of its thin population at the time, was comparable with that in 1906 [San Francisco], and various intensities were reported at roughly equal distances from the fault on the two occasions. The magnitudes of the two events cannot have differed greatly. . . . accounts . . . state that the ground opened in a great crack 40 miles long in the vicinity of Fort Tejon. This was an army post about 4 miles from the San Andreas fault, on the route of . . . US 99 between Los Angeles and San Francisco . . . Other reports place the southeastern end of visible displacements near San Bernardino . . ." (Richter 1958:475).

Tahquitz wayo na va (218)   Tahquitz (Lily) Rock
"Tahquitz standing"

Ca wis ke on ca, going up Chino Canyon made the signs of the trails: "Going hunting to the top of the mountains, he put the marks on the rocks. Near the top, at the spring , there is a large white rock standing by itself, nearly one thousand feet high. He called that great rock Tahquitz wayo na va, meaning Tahquitz standing" (Patencio 1943:96).

This rock is nearly a thousand feet high. It gets its English name from Lily Eastman, daughter of Dr. Sanford Eastman, first secretary and one of the original directors of the Southern California Colony Association which became Riverside. She died young of tuberculosis (Gunther 1984:291). See also (Gunther 1984:523-524).

Tama (Tu muli, Ta mare) (219)   Windy Point
"The mouth or opening of a pass"   Whitewater Point

"One of the head men came and stood on the Whitewater Point, called by the Indians *Tu muli*, and was watching the people choke up the pass in trying to get through" (Patencio 1943:100).

The great *net*, naming the places that marked his territory, came to three points in turn on his way north: ". . . the third point almost at Whitewater station, he called *tama*" (Strong 1929:101).

Evon ga net "went on to what is now Whitewater Point. He called that *Ta mare* meaning the mouth or opening of a pass" (Patencio 1943:54).

During the stagecoach days of the 1860s, "The next stop was at White Water Point. This is at the cut in the boulevard, by a small hill. . . . The corrals were cut back into the hill. Now it is all covered by white sand" (Patencio 1943:61).

This point is now known as Windy Point.

Tanki ? (220)   Sand Hole ?

According to Curtis, *Tanki* was "southward and around" the first point in the range east of Agua Caliente. The word may be derived from the "Mexican-Spanish *tanque*, water-hole." See *Kawis-ismal*, Cathedral City (Curtis 1926:164).

Bancroft in his 1863 "Guide To The Colorado Mines" describes an unreliable water hole, known as Sand Hole, about eleven miles southeast of Agua Caliente (Palm Springs). "This is a muddy pool about 400 yards east of the road, and which, as it consists only of a collection of rain-water in a small clay basin, is always bad, and dries up early in the summer. It is not to be depended upon except for a few months in the spring, and then only in case of a wet winter. There is little grass, of a poor quality, the only feed anywhere about" (Bancroft 1933:3-10). This tinaja may have located in the vicinity of Palm Desert (Johnston 1972:120; Gunther 1984:455-456).

From Palm Desert (west side at intersection of Hwys 111 and 74) to Agua Caliente is about 13.5 miles. A more likely location for Sand Hole is at the mouth of Magnesia Springs Canyon or the mouth of Bradley Canyon. Bradley Canyon is the most likely as the intermittent stream is within about 1/4 mile of the old road. An old article circa. 1930-40's, tells about people going to a spring? in Bradley. In addition Bradley Canyon is south and around the point from Cathedral Canyon.

Tatmilmi (165)   Palm Canyon Village

A village in Palm Canyon that was originally occupied by the *Atcitcem* lineage, Coyote moiety. It was given to the *Kauisiktum* lineage, with whom the *Atcitcem* usually intermarried, as a gift. The *Atcitcem* are also listed as living at *Kavinic*, Indian Wells, to which they may have moved at a later time, or which may have been a place from which they went to *Tatmilmi* on a seasonal basis (Strong 1929:91; Gifford 1918:191; Curtis 1926:163).

The great *net* "named . . . *tatmilmi* (the south end of Palm Canyon)" (Strong 1929:100).

Francisco Patencio told Strong that: "originally the *atcitcem* clan had owned Palm Canyon but as they usually married with the *kauisiktum* clan, they had given Palm Canyon to them as a gift. The old town located in the canyon, and once occupied by the *atcitcem* clan, was named *tatmilmi*" (Strong 1929:Ftnt. 179, 101).

A possible location for *Tatmilmi* is in the vicinity of Agua Bonita Spring in Palm Canyon.

Taupakic (221)   Cathedral Canyon

The great *net*, going southeast from Murray hill, "named *taupakic* (probably Cathedral Canyon, where they gathered mescal) . . ." (Strong 1929:101).

Tauvol-luk-a-let Kawis (222)   Thundering Rock

A rock in Chino Canyon. "Across from the Leaning Rock are put two large rocks. They are called the Hoof of the Rock and the Thundering Rock, two names" (Patencio 1943:73).

Near these two rocks on the trail below Leaning Rock are Hunter's Rock and "Place Of Resting" Rock and near the "Place Of Resting" Rock, Coyote and Wildcat Mortar Rocks (Patencio 1943:73, 98).

Ta vish mo (223)

Ca wis ke on ca, tracing *Kauisik* boundaries, "climbed the hill we called Lincoln Peak, and coming down part way he came to the place of paint and lime. This was used by the Indians for face paint. This he called *Ta vish mo*" (Patencio 1943:97).

Tcia (224)

The clan home of the *Tcianakiktum* lineage, Coyote moiety. This group was said to be extinct by the 1920s.

This village was west of the village of *Wiliya*. Strong's map (1929:145) places it north of Hot Springs Mountain and west and slightly south of *Wiliya*, i. e., south of the Riverside-San Diego county line and north of Lost Valley. This would place it near the head of the North Fork of Alder Canyon or between the North and South Forks of Alder Canyon.

Tcial (225)   Spitler Peak ?
"Head with feathers in hair"

The great *net*, proceeding northwestward "named *pinalata*, *kalahal* (a flat), *tcial* (a hill northwest of Palm Canyon) . . ." (Patencio 1943:100, Strong 1929).

It is assumed that this is a reference to a place northwest of the mouth of Palm Canyon. The great *net* is traveling from Indian Potrero (*Sim mo ta*) to Apache Spring and Ansell Rock (*Pul lo cla*).

Tciuk (226)

A place in the Santa Rosa Mountains from which the *Wakaikiktum* lineage came (Strong 1929:52).

Tehaukalumal (227)

The area to the east of the highway from La Mesa, across from the village of *Iltcuñaloñi* (Strong 1929:52, Ftnt.).

Tekelkukuaka (Tak el koko a ka) (228)   Palm Canyon, Entrance To

The great *net*, naming the places that marked his new territory went from the mouth of Andreas Canyon north along the eastern edge of the mountains bordering the desert, named ". . . *tekelkukuaka* (mesquite grove slightly to north), *kakwawit* (mouth of Tahquitz Canyon) . . ." (Strong 1929:101).

This mesquite grove is between the mouths of Andreas and Tahquitz Canyons at the turn of the boulevard where East Palm Canyon intersect South Palm Canyon. South Palm Canyon continues south until it intersects with Indian Canyon.

"Where the paved road now turns east to Indio, south of Palm Springs, are mesquite trees. . . . . This land is very good. It was used by the Indians for their crops . . . since the Indians came to the valley. The irrigation ditch came from the rise on the left of Tahquitz, and ran down onto the farming land below. . . . But one time (I was very small; I could not remember yet) there came such earthquakes as had not been known to any of the people. . . . Then it was that Tahquitz Creek went dry, and only ran water in the winter time . . . And so the Indians could not raise crops on the Mesquite land anymore" (Patencio 1943:57-58).

Tekic **(10)**   Andreas Canyon, Rock Art Site

Near the mouth of Andreas Canyon a great *net* "found some painted rocks called *tekic*" (Strong 1929:100, 101).

Tekic

Temalsēkalet **(229)**
"Earth crack"

This village was located about one-half mile south of where the Martinez Reservation buildings are, but not within reservation boundaries. The village had a well and "in several places the individual families carried on agriculture in a small way" (Strong 1929:48,51). It was the village of the *Autaatem* lineage, Wildcat moiety. This group moved from its original home at *Wilamū* to *Temalsēkalet*. Related to the *Awilem* lineage, they shared with them food-gathering territories near the ancestral home. They also had mesquite thickets around *Temalsēkalet* owned communally by all families of the group, and they practised agriculture at *Temalsēkalet*. Strong suggests these two groups may be branch lineages of the same original group (Strong, 1929:48, 51; Curtis 1926:163; Gifford 1918:190).

This village was located some 90 feet below sea level, about 130 feet below the high stand of ancient Lake Cahuilla.

Temal-wa-hish **(230)**   La Mesa
"Dry earth"

Barrows gives this as the name of a village at La Mesa, now the Augustine Indian Reservation, said to be "brushy area one mile south where the La Mesa people hunted rabbits" (Strong 1929:52, Ftnt.). Strong gives the name of the village at La Mesa as originally *Kelewutkwīikwinu*, and later as *Itcuñaloñī* (q.v.) (1929:52). Gifford gives *Ekwawinet* instead of *Kelewutkwīikwinu* (1918:190).

Temaña (231)
"Low place" (Gifford 1918:191)

A place listed by Gifford as the original home of the *Iswetum* and *Awalim* lineages, Wildcat moiety, both lineages being also known as *Temanakiktum* (1918:191). Strong gives the original home of the *Awilem* as *Wilamū* and the "clan home" of the *Iswitim* as *Pasīawha*. The *Iswitim* are also known as the *Tepamokiktum* (Strong 1929:41, 44-45, 146, 148). All three groups are wildcat moiety. Gifford's *Temanakiktum* may be Strong's *Tepaīyauicem*, a branch of the *Wīwaiīstam ("wiwaik* coyote-people), whose "clan home" was at *Tepaña* (Strong 1929:146, 148). See *Tepaña*.

Temelmekmekuka (232)
"Earth"

This village was occupied by the *Wantcauem*, who are said to have lived originally in the Santa Rosa Mountains, and who later, after a flash flood down Martinez Canyon destroyed some of their homes, moved to *Pūichekiva*, two miles away. They continued to harvest *Temelmekmekuk*, which was rich in mesquites and edible cacti (Strong 1929:44, 47-48).

Temelmekmekuka was located about three quarters of a mile west of the highway, opposite Martinez, where the Narbonne Ranch was in 1929, and about two miles from *Puichekiva* (Strong 1929:44, 47-48). The location of the Narbonne Ranch is uncertain, as is which location of the highway Strong was referring to. The old highway, shown on the 1901 Indio Special Map, passed through Martinez; so three-quarters of a mile west would place the village at or near the community of 100 Palms (middle of Section 17 or in the East 1/2 of Section 17) along present-day Highway 86. The elevation of the site would have been 80 feet below sea level and 120 feet below the high stand of ancient Lake Cahuilla.

If Strong was referring to present-day location of Highway 86, then village would have been located in the East 1/2 of Section 18 at an approximate elevation of 40 feet below sea level and 80 feet below the high stand of ancient Lake Cahuilla.

Temewhanvitcem Village (233)

A village occupied by the *Temewhanvitcem*, Coyote moiety, a lineage of the *Wīwaiīstam* clan. It was northeast of *Wilīya*, their clan home (Strong 1929:145,146, 148).

The site of this village was possibly at the west end of the Middle Willows in Coyote Canyon. The Middle Willows is the continuation of a riparian area along Coyote Creek, the only permanently running stream in San Diego County. Along this water course are stands of wash willows, palms, cottonwoods, and unfortunately now, salt cedar. Above Middle Willows are stands of Mohave yucca, juniper trees, cottonwood, oak and alder groves in the upstream tributary canyons of Coyote Canyon. "Yucca Valley . . . extends south from the west side of Middle Willows." Climbing from the valley floor into the mountains, one passes through creosote, juniper, yucca and squaw tea (Lindsay and Lindsay 1984:93,104).

Tem ma ves el (234)

A place in a wash where there was a great deal of sediment near which there was a mesquite grove. *Ca wis ke on ca*, having left the Garnet hills, and the place a mile up the wash "where the white flowers grow", coming "west, toward Palm Springs about a mile, he called that place *Tem ma ves el*, which means sediment. The mesquites which grew thick at the turn of the boulevard . . ." (Patencio 1943:99).

It appears that this site was in Palm Canyon Wash. At this point *Ca wis ke on ca* is about 1 mile west of the confluence of Palm Canyon and Tahquitz Canyon washes, about 2 miles from the mouth of Eagle Canyon, in the wedge of land between the two washes. This wedge is north of the Araby Tract and East Palm Canyon Boulevard (Highway 111) and south of Tahquitz wash, in and around El Cielo Avenue. Palm Canyon wash crosses under East Palm Canyon Boulevard (Hwy 111) at the bridge by Rim Road and Southridge Drive. Tahquitz wash crosses El Cielo about one half-mile south of Ramon Avenue.

Temukvaal (235)

The great *net*, going north from the mouth of Andreas Canyon, . . ."named . . . *temukvaal* (a low hill on edge of desert near here where a man watched when they hunted rabbits), *tekelkukuaka* (mesquite grove slightly to the north . . .)" (Strong 1929:101).

Francisco Patencio notes: "Where the paved road now turns east to Indio, south of Palm Springs, are mesquite trees" (Patencio 1943:57-58). This mesquite grew at the turn of the boulevard where South Palm Canyon intersects East Palm Canyon Boulevard (Hwy 111 curves eastward). The low hill is north of the mouth of Andreas Canyon and south of the turn of the boulevard at the base of the San Jacinto Mountains. It is probably the hill up which Cantina Way and Cahuilla Hills Drive climb. These streets are just north of Canyon Vista.

Tepal (138)

The great *net*, proceeding to the north from Tahquitz Falls, "named *invitca* (a green place north of Tahquitz Canyon), *tepal* (farther north) . . ." (Strong 1929:101)

This is perhaps one of several tinajas in the small canyon at the end of Barristo Road at Tahquitz Drive to the left of the main building of the Palm Springs Tennis Club. *Tepal* is possibly the same place as *Pa cale* (q.v.).

Tepaña (236)

This village was occupied by the *Tepaiyauitcem*, a lineage of the *Wiwaiistam* clan, Coyote moiety (Strong 1929:146, 148).

According to Strong's map (1929:145), this outlying village of the *Wiwaiistam* people was probably located near the village of *Wiliya* in lower Alder Canyon, possibly where the north and south forks of the canyon join. Alder Canyon is a tributary canyon of Coyote Canyon. See note below; also see *Wiliya* (Strong 1929:146, 148).

"Seasonal streams ripple down both forks of Alder to join the tree-shaded grove where old cottonwood trees are found. Alders may be found upstream of these old cottonwoods. . . .Vegetation in this canyon is indicative of higher elevation and changing life zone. Juniper, scrub oak, white sage, Mohave yucca, and mangalar sumac are found in addition to buckhorn cholla, desert apricot, goatnut and catclaw" (Lindsay and Lindsay 1984:94-95).

According to the Lindsays, the Cahuilla village of *Tepaña* was located in Tule Canyon (Lindsay and Lindsay 1984:96). This disagrees with Strong's map (p. 145) which places *Tepaña* in Alder Canyon. *Tepaña* may be the same place as *Temaña*.

Tep po we (237)   Garnet Ridge & Tank
"A water tank"

Evon ga net "followed down the ridge and came to a place which he named *tep po we*, a water tank. This is a very large hollow rock on top of the ridge; it is nearly always filled with water, and can be seen for many miles around. Then he came down near to what is now called Palm Canyon" (Patencio 1943:53).

Schwenn notes that *Evon ga net* went from Cedar Spring and Palm View Peak down the ridge to Indian Potrero. There are 3 ridges radiating from Palm View Peak--Garnet Ridge, Bald Mountain-Hell's Kitchen Ridge, and the Desert Divide. On the northwest side of Palm View Peak is Garnet

Ridge. The old Indian Trail from Cedar Springs went northward to Little Camp Spring and down the upper portion of Garnet Ridge at which point it dropped northwestward into the West Fork of Palm Canyon near Agua Fuerte Spring. Continuing down the ridge, one could descend into Bullseye Flat along Cedar Creek and the Indian Potrero. The Hell's Kitchen Trail descends the ridge by Little Desert Peak, southeast of Palm View Peak, toward Bald Mountain. Bald Mountain has large rocks on it and is about 1 mile south of Indian Potrero. The Hell's Kitchen Trail was constructed by the CCC, but may have been an earlier Cahuilla trail. The Desert Divide (Pacific Crest Trail) continues southeast from Palm View Peak, but there is no known tinaja along this ridge unless there is one on Pine Mountain which has a large rock on it that can be seen from many points in Palm Canyon.

Tep ush ha (Tep ush la) (238)

A sharp hill between Banning and Beaumont, ". . . place was once owned by a Mexican named Miguel Hagaira, and is now known as the Hagaira Poterio" (Patencio 1943:100).

Tetcanaakiktum (239)   Snow Creek Village
"Place name for peak south of the Pass"
A village near the mouth of Snow Creek, occupied by the *Tetcanaakiktum* lineage, Coyote moiety (Strong 1929:91). The peak from which the village took its name may be Black Mountain.

Tetcavi (240)

"Proceeding still to the north, he [the great *net*] named . . . *tetcavi* (a large rock fifty yards farther north)" (Strong 1929:101).
This rock is located on the point (*To e ve val* or *Tuival*) behind the Palm Springs Desert Museum, between the west ends of Tahquitz Way and Chino Drive.

Teūamul (241)   South Point, Blaisdell Canyon

The great *net*, going north from Chino Canyon, "named . . . *kistcavel* (at point where second bridge on highway from Palm Springs to Whitewater is located). The first rocky point beyond this bridge he [great *net*] called *pīonvil*, the second point *teūamul* . . ." (Strong 1929:101).
Between Chino Canyon and Windy Point are three points--*Malal*, the north point of Chino Canyon; *Kish chowl* (or *Kistcavel*), the point between *Malal* and the south point of Blaisdell Canyon; and *Ta was ah mo* (or *Teūamul*), the south point of Blaisdell Canyon. This is the point before Windy Point and the second point beyond the second bridge. This point is about 0.4 mile southwest of Overture Drive on Highway 111 and northeast of Desert Angel. Whitewater Point is an older name for Windy Point.

Tev ing el we wy wen it (Tēvin' imulwinwaīwinut) (242)
"A round flat basket closed up at the top, that is hung up."
The son of *Ca wis ke on ca* moved to this place near the mouth of Palm Canyon and raised a large family (Patencio 1943:90).
The great *net* named "*tēvin' imulwiwaīwinut* (a flat rock with mortar holes) at the mouth of Palm Canyon . . . " (Strong 1929:100).
The mouth of Palm Canyon is located just north of Hermit's Bench where the east and west forks join. The *Panyik* village, later called Rincon, was located here.

Tevutt (Tevi) (243,20)
"The place of the pinyon trees"

This village was located on Little Pinyon Flats, near Cactus Springs?, the lower of two villages on the flats. "The sites of both *Weh-ghett* and *Tev-utt* contain many bedrock mortar grinding places, smooth rock floors where people used to dance, and many pictographs and petroglyphs (Modesto 1978).

Strong gives *Tevi*, "round basket," as the original home of the *Tevinakiktum*, Wildcat moiety, who later lived at *Palpunivikiktum hemki* at Alamo (1929:41). Gifford identifies this group as belonging to the Coyote moiety (1918:191).

There are four trails diverging from near Cactus Springs, the Cactus Springs trail heads east and west from the spring, the *Tukut* (old Guadalupe Trail) turns northeast toward modern Lake Cahuilla and La Quinta, and a fourth trail (Vandeventer?) turns south toward Santa Rosa Mountain.

Three Buttes (174,141,244)
Salton Sea

"There are several small islands, or hills when the water is not there, at the end of the Salton Sea" (Patencio 1943:85).

"When the ocean was gone and the valley was dry land, the Indians went to the Three Buttes-- Mullet Island, the largest hill, and Paint and Pelican Island--the next in size. Here they broke off pieces of flint or volcanic glass to make arrow point and knives" (Patencio 1971:17-18).

See also Paint Island and Pelican Island.

To ba (245)   Travertine Palms Spring
"A small tree that has an oily seed, much like a coffee bean. The tree grows there [at the spring]."

"The Santa Rosa range runs down east to a point where there is a spring--*To ba*. Here the Indian people lived for many, many years. Not the first created people, but the tribe of *Cow nuk kal kik tem*. They did not live right at the spring, but about ten miles beyond it" (Patencio 1943:113).

The *Kaunukalkiktum* (*Cow nuk kal kik tem*) Cahuilla lived at *Īviatim* Village (near present day Agua Dulce) (Strong 1929:42). Travertine Palms and a spring, now dry, are located nearly 400 feet above sea level in the third "bay" southwest of Travertine Point about 3/4 mile west of the San Diego-Imperial County line and 1-3/4 miles south of the Riverside-Imperial County line. The high water line of ancient Lake Cahuilla was about 40 feet above sea level. A major trail runs from Garnet Wash to Travertine Palms to Wonderstone Wash and across the divide to Palo Verde Wash. From Palo Verde Wash other trails lead to Coyote Canyon, Font's Point, and Clark Valley.

The plant, *To ba*, may be the desert shrub jojoba (*Simmondsia chinensis*, Family *Buxaceae*), also known as goatnut. Jojoba is a tall shrub (up to 2 meters high) with thick leathery leaves known for its long life (up to 100 years) and its fruit, containing an oily, but edible seed. The seeds can be made into a rich drink and also yield a commercially desirable oil, chemically, a liquid wax. Found along the desert margin below 5,000 feet, jojoba prefers to grow on dry rocky slopes.

To e ve val (Tūīval) (246)
"Place of grinding"

Ca wis ke on ca "went to the point where Bishop and Meade have built winter houses. "There were seven mortars made in the rock, but these grinding holes were blasted out in the Whitewater irrigating ditch" (Patencio 1943:98).

The great *net*, moving northward, "named . . . a green place north of Tahquitz Canyon, . . . *tūīval* (a rocky point just west of the Mission Inn) . . ." (Strong 1929:101).

This is the point behind the Palm Springs Desert Museum, between the west ends of Tahquitz Way and Chino Drive.

According to one source, the Bishop and Meade homes are both still standing on West Tahquitz Way at 412 W. Tahquitz Way and 468 W. Tahquitz Way, respectively.

The Whitewater irrigation ditch joined the Tahquitz ditch in the vicinity of the O'Donnel Golf Course. See entry, "Irrigation Ditch, Tahquitz Canyon."

The rocky point described above is that point of the San Jacinto Mountains between the west end of Tahquitz Way and the west end of Chino Drives. This is the point behind (west of) the new Palm Springs Desert Museum and the O'Donnell Golf Course, the point south of Tachevah Canyon. The South Lykken Trail climbs to the summit of this point where it merges with the Museum Trail at the picnic tables.

There is now no Mission Inn in Palm Springs; however the old Desert Inn on the southwest corner of Palm Canyon and Tahquitz Way looked somewhat like a mission. The other, less likely, candidate is the old El Mirador Hotel, located on the site of the present Desert Hospital on North Indian Avenue between El Mirador and Tachevah.

To-ho (Tohoo) (247)   Deep Canyon

"Hunter who never gets his game" (Chase 1919:30).

This canyon is important in Cahuilla sacred literature as the home of Yellow Body (Patencio 1943:37), and as an occupied area. It was the site of a village at some time in the past, and has enormous floral and faunal potential.

According to Curtis, *Tohoo* was "in the curve of the mountains between *Tanki* and Indian Wells." *Tanki* was "southward and around" the first point in the range east of Agua Caliente. See *Kawis-ismal* and *Tanki*, Sand Hole (Curtis 1926:164).

Tong wen nev al (248)

"The place of wasted mescal"

Ca wis ke on ca "came down to the foothills, to the place where the water of Tahquitz turns into the Indian ditch today, and he called it *Tong wen nev al* . . ." (Patencio 1943:97).

There were two irrigation ditches from Tahquitz. One ran from the mouth of Tahquitz to the turn of the boulevard and then toward the old townsite of Palmdale. "The irrigation ditch came from the rise on the left of Tahquitz and ran down onto the farming land below. This old ditch was used so much that today it looks like a small dry creek bed" (Patencio 1943:57-58). The other irrigation ditch ran northward from the mouth of Tahquitz Canyon near the gaging station to the point of the mountains at the end of Tahquitz Way, joining the Whitewater irrigation ditch near the south end of the O'Donnell Golf Course.

To quo a (249)   Deer Springs ?

"Mountain lion"

A spring *Evon ga net* formed on top of a mountain (Patencio 1943:52).

One possible spring is Deer Springs, located at nearly 10,000 feet, northwest of Marion Mountain and south-southwest of Mount San Jacinto. Mount San Jacinto, Jean Peak and Marion Peak form a long ridge between the Idyllwild area and the desert.

Torro See *Mauūlmii*.

Torro Cemetery (121)

This cemetery is associated with *Toro* (Torres Martinez Reservation). Members of the *Waikaiktum* are buried generally in the western part of the cemetery; members of the Levi family in the center, and of the Duros from Santa Rosa in the eastern part of it, according to Alice Lopez.

Torro Wells (121)

The Cahuilla built walk-in wells to provide themselves with a water supply before contact with Europeans. They continued to dig such wells after contact. In the late 19th century there were eight wells at *Toro*, at that time used for irrigation of mesquite and other food plants. Some of the wells survived at least into the 1930s (Barrows 1900:26-27; Baldwin 1938).

Trail between Nicolas (Nicholias) Canyon and Santa Rosa Reservation (250)

Reed says, "Of the old Indian trails leading to and from Rockhouse Valley is one between the present Santa Rosa Reservation and Nicolas Canyon that is still used by persons going to or from Rockhouse on foot or on horseback" (1963:126).

Trail from Box Canyon to Hidden Spring (252)

"A trail leading from near the mouth of Coyote Canyon to Hidden Spring can still be followed; starting up North Canyon (Box Canyon) for about a mile, then up small side canyon for about the same distance to where the trail turns sharply to the right across several rocky ridges, then into some little valley-like places where the water stands for quite some time after heavy rainfall. Here again is evidence of the Indians having taken advantage of times when water was available for their camps while gathering food" (Reed 1963:113-114).

Trail from Clark Dry Lake to Rabbit Peak (251)

This trail goes up steeply from the site of Clark Lake Dune village to an elevation of 5000 feet in the course of four miles, ending on Rabbit Peak. There are numerous olla sherds on the way.

Trail from Coyote Canyon/Borrego Valley to Clark Lake and Hidden Spring (253)

"An Indian trail that is still easy to follow whenever it was not in the sand washes, leads into the Clark Lake area, with a branch leading to Hidden Spring. This trail comes across a rough ridge extending to the north from Butler Mountain, and was used by the Clark brothers when taking supplies to their cow-camp. This trail starts across this rough ridge directly across the valley from the Doc Beaty Place (Anza Ranch)" (Reed 1963:116).

The 1901 Indio Quadrangle (Topo) shows a trail leading from the Coyote Canyon-Borrego Valley across Alcoholic Pass (not named until later topo) to Clark Valley. From there the trail branches east toward Clark Lake and northwest to Hidden Springs. Schad states that travel over Alcoholic Pass is an old Cahuilla trail. "For centuries Indians used Alcoholic Pass as a convenient short cut between Coyote Canyon and Clark Valley. In time, a well-beaten trail was worn across the precipitous slopes west of the pass. Around the turn of the century, the Clark brothers, early cattlemen who homesteaded in Coyote Canyon, used this trail to transport some primitive well-drilling equipment to the site now known as Clarks Well in Clark Valley. Near the top of the pass, the old Indian Trail squeezed between two boulders so closely spaced that the burros had to be unpacked before going through" (Schad 1986:194). Butler is not shown on the topo.

Trail from Horse Canyon to Hidden Spring (254)

Reed described a trail that led from Coyote Canyon to the Santa Rosa Reservation. "A branch from this trail leading from the water in Horse Canyon across the mountain in a south-easterly direction to Hidden Spring, Clark Lake, and into the Rockhouse Valley areas. Along this branch of the trail are evidences of many of the mescal pits" (Reed 1963:111-112).

It would be necessary to walk this trail to locate it precisely.

Trail from Middle Willows to Hidden Spring (255)

Reed describes a trail from Middle Willows, "across the rugged mountain to the east is another one of the Indians' travel-ways leading to Hidden Spring. . ... Along this trail after one travels across the rough mountains, there is considerable evidence of the Indians having lived there, at least when gathering food. Near the larger granite boulders can be found small pieces of broken pottery and signs of mescal pits" (1963:113).

It would be necessary to walk this trail to locate it precisely.

Trail from Rockhouse Valley to Toro Peak (256)

"The old trail leading from Rockhouse Valley to the north on Toro Peak is said to be extremely difficult because of its not being used and due to heavy rains that have fallen through the years" (Reed 1963:126). Reed does not give any more information about the location of this trail.
This trail ends in or near Nicholias Canyon, where there is a pictograph on the canyon wall.

Trail in Rockhouse Valley (257)

This trail went between two villages in Rockhouse Valley. These were old village sites.

Trail Shrines (258)

"All trails were kept clear by the Indians. When the hunters were having trouble about things, they gathered up rocks from the trail, and put them in piles on the side. This pleased the spirits, and caused good will" (Patencio 1943:73).

There are trail shrines along the trail in Palm Canyon near the south end of Indian Potrero. Other locations include the old Cahuilla Trail from Thousand Palms to Hidden Palms and the *Isil* Trail from the mouth of Bear Creek Canyon, La Quinta, to Deep Canyon. The latter trail follows the Coyote Creek and Bear Creek drainages.

Travertine Point (259)

Point west of the Salton Sea where Eagle Flower's youngest son and his mother settled for a time: "Before they reached the point his first child, a son, was born. He [Eagle Flower's youngest son] made a cave in the hill, and he, his wife and his mother lived there" (Patencio 1943:43).

"During the existence of Lake Cahuilla, Travertine Point was a low-lying semicircular group of hills which extended 0.8 km from the mountains. Travertine Rock, the hill farthest from the mountains, was never submerged by the lake but formed a small island rising a few meters above the water" (Theilig, Womer & Papson 1978:117). The highest stand of the lake was between 25 to 60 feet above sea level.

Travertine Rocks Cave and Petroglyphs (260)

The travertine rocks are the remains of an ancient island, covered with a thick layer of calcium carbonate, the remains of the shells of marine animals. Chase found a cave on the northeast side of this outcrop, about 60 feet deep, and containing pottery sherds, but no traces of smoke on the ceiling and minimal plant life. He interpreted these details to mean the cave was a place of refuge (1919:186).

Steward described petroglyphs on the rocks. They are carved in the travertine, and dated from various periods. Some appeared to have been carved before the last rise of Lake Cahuilla. One bore the date "1898" carved in the travertine. Plain pottery sherds were found at the western base of the rocks (1929:87).

Tūikiktumhemkī (261)

A village occupied by the *Tūikiktum* lineage, Wildcat moiety. Their food-gathering territory was in the canyons to the east of the village, probably in the Mecca Hills, rather than the Little San Bernardinos as Strong suggests. This group was subordinate to the *Kauwicpaumēauitcem*, Cabezon's clan, who lived at *Maswut Helaanut*, Painted Canyon (Strong 1929:41, 54).

Tūikiktumhemkī was located just east of the Southern Pacific railroad line half way between Mecca and Thermal. The village would have been located west of the mouth of Painted Canyon, possibly on the Cabezon Reservation in Section 6, T6S, SBBM.

This village was located at about 150 feet below sea level; so it would have been some 190 feet below the high stand of ancient Lake Cahuilla.

Tukut (262)   "Old Guadalupe Trail"
"Wild cat"

This major trail ran along the northern portion of the south fork of this creek from the La Quinta area to Little Pinyon Flat in the Santa Rosa Mountains.

Tukut kaw-we-vah-ah (263)   Wildcat Mortar Rock
"Wildcat Mortar Rock"

Close to *Num na sh b al*, "Place Of Resting Rock", "are two large rocks which have small mortar holes in them, not more than three inches across. These small holes were never used for grinding, but to make the sign of the trail. One is called the coyote mortar rock . . . The other is called the wild cat mortar rock, and has a shallow hole" (Patencio 1943:98).

Coyote and Wildcat Mortar Rocks are near the "Place Of Resting" Rock. The latter rock stands by the old Cahuilla trail from Palm Springs to Chino Canyon near the boundary sign on the south point of Chino Canyon. Another small rock near the trail is the Hunter's Rock which is located in Chino Canyon below Leaning Rock, probably on the north side of the south point of Chino Canyon (Patencio 1943:73).

Tūrka (264)

Tūrka was one of the places owned by the *Mariñga* clan of Serranos. It was in "Morongo Valley, along the present road" (Benedict 1924:368). Its exact location is unknown.

Fig Tree John at his home at *Tuva*

Tūva (265)

This village on the shores of the Salton Sea was the home, originally, of the *Telakiktum* lineage, Coyote moiety, before the historic period. Its members were all dead "when informants first remembered the place." In the late nineteenth century, it was the home of the *Wantciñakik Tamīanwitcem* lineage, the lineage of Juan Razon, better known as Fig Tree John. The spring at *Tūva* had water enough for domestic purposes, but not enough for irrigation. This spring was known as Fish Springs. *Tūva* is presently inundated by the Salton Sea.

"Then he [*Aswitseī*, Eagle Flower] found the tracks of his wife and mother-in-law. The former had had another child while she was running away [from *Kōtevewit*]. So they all wept together and settled at *Tūva* (near Agua Dulce)" (Strong 1929:86).

Possibly now under water or adjacent to the Salton Sea, Fish Springs was located where Desert Shores now stands in Section 9 or 10, T9S, R9E, about one and one-half miles south of the Riverside-Imperial county line and two and one-half to three miles east of the San Diego-Imperial county line. At 230 feet below sea level, the location would have been some 270 feet below the high stand of ancient Lake Cahuilla (40 feet above sea level).

Ūakī (266)

A village in the Santa Rosa Mountains that was the original home of the *Wīitem* lineage, Coyote moiety, who later moved to *Pal hīliwit* near Martinez (Strong 1929:42, 51).

"*Wīitam* is said to mean 'grasshopper,' a name applied to this clan because of the habit of eating grasshoppers." Gifford suggests that this group may perhaps be the same as the *Wiyistam* group at San Ysidro (1918:191). The specific location of *Ūakī* is not known.

Ulicpatciat (267)

The site of a prehistoric village on the shore of the Salton Sea: "Near *Tūva*, at a place called *ūlicpatciat*, a clan called *mūmūkwitcem* (always sick) lived before Francisco remembers; he was told of them, but they, like the *telakiktum* people, were all dead before he was born" (Strong 1972:49).

After their headman was killed by the mountain lion on Mount San Jacinto, the *Mo Moh Pechem* ("moaning in pain") people walked down to Palm Canyon. "These people lived on the mountains, and called themselves *Mo moh pechem* . . . The people prayed, and flew again to the end of the Santa Rosa range. Here they found many small shells, and they called it the place of the shells" (Patencio 1943:32-34).

From the end of the Santa Rosas, the *Mo Moh Pechem* flew to "another open place on the plain" in the San Felipe Valley and here the animal, *To quastto hut*, took 2 or 3 people every day (Patencio 1943:34). *Esel i hut* "went to the end of the Santa Rosa Range, to the place of the *Mo moh pechem* people. There he found a large village of many houses . . . but the whole place was wiped out by the *To quassto hot*, the sky animal that was eating two and three of the people every day" (Patencio 1943:35).

"At the first village he came to, he [*Tukvachtahat*] saw a great many houses by they were all deserted . . . At the last house in the village, he found two old women. These women who very much frightened when they saw *Tukvachtahat*. He asked them why, and they said, 'There is a wild man around here who has been capturing two of the village people every day, taking them away with him, and then eating them'" (Hooper 1920:369-370).

Virgin Spring and Trail (268)

This spring is to the west of Toro Peak. It lies on an important trail which leads westward down the mountain and then north to Palm Canyon.

Wa wash ca le it (269)   Murray Hills

"The Murray Hills are full of Indian trails. . . . A trail crosses the Murray Hills from the Garden of Eden. It passes Eagle Spring and some others on the way east to Indian Wells -- Magnesia Canyon, Cathedral Canyon (Patencio 1943:71; 1971:16).

Evon ga net "came to the next point which he called *Wa wash ca le it* . . . . These are now known as the Murray Hills, and the same stripes or streaks are there today" (Patencio 1943:53).

This is the second point, north of Palm Canyon, along the western edge of the Murray Hills (Santa Rosa foothills). Opposite (east of) the mouth of *Os Wit* Canyon, in the Palm Canyon Wash, *Wa wash ca le it* is just north of the bridge on Bogart Trail and on the north side of Andreas Cove. The Araby Tract and Hawk Canyon are north and east from this point in Palm Canyon wash; the next point to the northeast is Song Point (where Palm Canyon wash crosses beneath Highway 111). See Hawk Canyon and Song Point. While there are no "stripes" on the point itself, the slopes to the south behind Andreas Cove, are streaked by bands of white crystalline limestone beds. The Garstin Trail climbs from the tip of the point eastward and upward to the summit of Smoke Tree Mountain. See also *Sewitckul*. The Theleman Trail climbs from Andreas Cove to the base of Wildhorse Ridge joining there trails to Eagle Canyon, Murray Peak and Deep Canyon.

Waīvas (270)   Leaning Rock
"Yell" "Screaming'

". . . still farther in the same direction [north] he [great *net*] named a hanging rock *waīvas* . . ." (Strong 1929:101).

"In coming to Palm Springs, or leaving it, there is to be noticed a great leaning rock on the hillside entering Chino Canyon. . . . This is a medicine rock. It is a medicine rock to love, to cure too, but most to love. The medicine under the Leaning Rock is made of everything that the people and the animals love. Honey for the bears, nuts for the squirrels, seed for the birds, so many things make the medicine that is put there. . . . It [Leaning Rock] sits on a great flat rock that makes a tipped-up platform, and on this the great Medicine Rock sets" (Patencio 1943:72-73).

Leaning Rock stands on the hillside, south point of Chino Canyon near the end of the paved section of Chino Canyon Road. Chino Canyon Road is part of the old wagon road that once climbed into the canyon. The wagon road continues from the end of the paved section to about the first curve in Tramway Drive where it disappears beneath the paved road. It has been assumed here that the hanging rock *waivas* and Leaning Rock are the same rock. Other nearby rocks include Hunter's Rock, Coyote and Wildcat Mortar Rocks, Thundering Rock, Hoof of the Rock, and the Three Large Rocks At Or Near Chino South.

Wakaxix (Waki, Wakihe) (271)   Blaisdell Canyon Village

Blaisdell Canyon north of Cabezon, the territory of the *Wakiñakiktum* lineage of the *Wanikik* clan, which occupied the San Gorgonio Pass (Strong 1929:91; Bean 1960). Benedict gives Wakatit as the Serrano name for the area (1924).

Wani (Wanup, Wanet) (272)   Whitewater River, Mouth of
"Running water"

"*Wanup*" is the Cahuilla name for the mouth of Whitewater Canyon (Benedict 1924:112).
"*Wani* is the district south of San Gorgonio pass" (Curtis 1926:164).
The *Wanakik* lineage of the *Wanakik* clan, Coyote moiety, lived originally at *Wani*, moving later to *Malki* (Bean 1960).

Wantciña (118)   Martinez Mountain

This mountain in the Santa Rosas from which the *Wantciñakiktum* take their name was a major area for Cahuilla hunting, gathering, and sacred activity. The *Wantciñakiktum* at one time lived in Martinez Canyon at *Īsilsiveyauitcem* (Strong 1929:41, 44, 50).

Watcicpa (273)   Redlands Junction

"Very long ago a great *net* . . . brought his people to *watcicpa* (Redland Junction)" (Strong 1929:100).

Wavaai ? (274)   Fargo (Rockhouse) Canyon

Strong states that the *Wavaaīkiktum* group took its name from a canyon in the Little San Bernardino Mountains to the east of the village of *Paltēwat*, near Indio (Strong 1929:42, 56). Several canyons cut through the Little San Bernardinos east of Indio, the largest of which is Fargo Canyon. Fargo Canyon heads northeast into the Little San Bernardinos, forking about three miles from the canyon mouth. The left fork, called Rockhouse Canyon, trends northward and drains the Pleasant Valley area in Joshua Tree National Monument; and the right fork, called Fargo Canyon, bends toward the east.

Weh-ghett (20,275)
"Place of the Ponderosa Pines"

This village was located on Little Pinyon Flats, on the north side of Santa Rosa Mountain. It was the higher of two villages, the other being *Tev-utt* on the Flat.

The sites of both *Weh-ghett* and *Tev-utt* contain many bedrock mortar grinding places, smooth rock floors where people used to dance, and many pictographs and petroglyphs (Modesto 1978). This is probably the same village as *We-wut now hu* (q.v.)

West Fork, Palm Canyon Hunting Trail (276)

This hunting trail led up the west fork of Palm Canyon. Agua Fuerte Spring was the source of water in the canyon. The trail also led past another spring east of the canyon, Agua Caliente, Indian Spring.

We-wut now hu (206)   New Santa Rosa
"In the middle of the pine"

One of the names of New Santa Rosa (Barrows 1900:37), which was otherwise known as *Sēwiū* (Strong 1929:145, 148, 151, 158). May be the same villages as *Weh-ghett* (q.v.).

Wiasmul (277)

A village to which the *Hōkwitcakiktum* moved from their clan home at *Hōkwitca*, and the *Apapatcem* from *Saupalpa*. Both were Wildcat moiety, and were probably lineages of one clan (Strong 1929:147, 148).

Wīasmul "was located at a small sulphur spring about four miles southwest of Cahuilla, *Pauī* (Strong 1929:145,147,148).

Wīasmul, shown on Strong's map, "was located at a small sulphur spring about four miles southwest of Cahuilla, *Pauī* (Strong 1929:145,147,379).

There are three springs southwest of Cahuilla (*Pauī*). The first two, located close together, on the south side of Cahuilla Creek near the base of the hills (Section 26) on the Cahuilla Reservation. The third spring is on the north side of the highway on the Reservation boundary near Lake Riverside and about 4 miles southwest of Cahuilla (Section 33, T7S, R2E). There are graves (marked on the topo) near the latter spring. The area along Cahuilla Creek, in the Cahuilla Valley, near the first two springs is a grassy cienaga with surface water.

Wilamū (Weal um mo?) (278)

A village in Martinez Canyon, possibly at Pinyon Alta Flat (Strong 1929:41).

It was the original home of the *Awilem*. They lived there with the *Autaatem* who were regarded as their relatives. From *Wilamū* they moved to Martinez, *Pūichekiva* but they retained their food-gathering territories near the older village. Strong suggests that both groups may be branch lineages of the same original group (Strong 1929:44-45, 48).

Here (on top of Santa Rosa Mountain) Yellow Body took a thorn from his foot. "This he threw on the top of a great rock. The thorn lay there for a time, and started to grow, and continues growing there. He called that mountain *Weal um mo*" (Patencio 1943:38).

Wilamu and *Weal um mo* are apparently the same term. The village at Pinyon Flat may have taken its name from the name of the nearby mountain top.

Wiliya (Wiwaiistam) (279)

This is the central village in Coyote Canyon which, according to Strong's map (1929:145), would have been located just west of the Middle Willows, in Fig Tree Valley, possibly near Bailey's Cabin or near the spring on the east side of Fig Tree Valley. It was occupied by the *Wiwaiistam*, Coyote moiety, whose clan home it was was. Several lineages of this group lived at or near this village, the *Nauhañavitcem* just to the south (possibly at Mangalar Spring) and the *Temewhanvitcem* to the northeast (possibly at Middle Willows). After the smallpox epidemic in the late 1870's the surviving members of the group moved to San Ignacio (or San Ysidro? Strong lists both locations) (Strong 1929:146, 148).

"Anza's camp on Christmas Eve 1775 was made at or near *Wiliya*. He called the Indians at the village Los Danzantes (The Dancers) because of these Indians' peculiar mannerisms of jumping, slapping their thighs and jerking while communicating with the Spaniards" (Lindsay and Lindsay 1984:94).

Woh hut cli a low win it (280)
"Pine tree mistletoe"

"Then he [*Ka wis ke on ca*] came to the place of the lone pine tree. He called that *Woh hut cli a low win it.* . . From there the trail separated, one going down what is now the Gordon (Palm to Pines) Trail, and the other coming down the ridge of the Tahquitz Canyon" (Patencio 1943:97).

The junction of the Gordon trail with the trail into Tahquitz Canyon is on the south ridge of Tahquitz Canyon below Caramba Camp at about 5,200 feet elevation.

Wonderstone Trail (293)

This trail leads from Palo Verde Wash to the Natural Rock Tanks in the Santa Rosa Mountains, thence to Wonderstone Wash and the Salton Sea. The rock tanks apparently were a great attraction for mountain sheep, and there are many sheep trails leading to them. Going further on this trail, Reed found another small tank near the trail. There were mescal pits, and other signs of an Indian camp site beside the tank. Across the main ridge of the mountains he found indications of two other camp sites showing signs of Indian habitation. He also found two rock cairns and several metates along the trail, and believes it was once "one of the main travel ways to the Salton Sea area" (Reed 1963:116-118).

Yamisevul (124)   Mission Creek Area

Originally a site used by the *Wanikik* Cahuilla, later occupied by Serrano who intermarried with the Wanikik Cahuilla, and later moved to present-day Morongo. *Yamisevul* was later occupied by Chemehuevi, and more recently by Luiseño. The Cahuilla name for the Serrano clan was *Marongam* (Gifford 1918:179). This aboriginal territory should not be confused with Mission Creek Indian Reservation of the historical period. Benedict reports that the Serrano name for the site of the *Marongam* village was *Yamisevul*, meaning "where the yucca blossoms," and says that it was at the canyon mouth of Mission Creek. The clan also owned the territory at *Maringa* and *Turka* (in Morongo Valley along the road in 1924) (Benedict 1924:368). The nature of aboriginal occupancy in this entire area is not well remembered by contemporary Serranos.

Yan heck e (281)
"Hole in the wind"

"This small hole is about two inches across, always has a breeze blowing through it, and has a rim of bright green grass which is always covered with dew." This hole is part way down from Lincoln Peak, on the west side of Tahquitz Canyon, "crossing a short way," probably on the trail from Caramba (upper Tahquitz) to the mouth of Tahquitz Canyon (Patencio 1943:973).

The exact location of this place is not known, but from the description of *Ca wis ke on ca*'s travels, it would be on the ridge heading southwest from Lincoln Peak (Elev.3808"). This ridge forms the north wall of Tahquitz Canyon.

Yauahic (282)

This is "a place just south of Blaisdell Canyon." The boundary could possibly be the 4800' high point in Section 2 south of Blaisdell Canyon or the 7600' high point in Section 11 southwest of Blaisdell (Strong 1929:101).

A hunting and friendship trail crossed the hills from Chino to Snow Creek passing by a spring above the green spot (spring at about 2320') which can be seen from Highway 111. Here Cahuilla women gathered wild plums (Patencio 1943:70).

You koo hul ya me (283)   Bullseye Rock
"The place of many brains"

"This big rock stands there today." After a battle at Seven Palms, "the heads of the chiefs and the head men and others [of Seven Palms people] of any importance were cut off and brought to Palm Springs in nets. The older men carried the heads to Palm Canyon, to a place now called Indian Potrero, above the mesquite trees. Here they were broken against a big rock and the brains taken out" (Patencio 1943:89).

Bullseye Rock is the large rock monolith along Cedar Creek between Indian Portrero and Bullseye Flat.

Young ga vet wit ham pah va (285)   Snow Creek Headwall
"The drinking place of the wild buzzards"

"Going to the high peak where the sun sets . . . Down below, where water runs in the canyon, that place he called *Young ga vet wit ham pah va*, which means the drinking place of the wild buzzards" (Patencio 1943:96).

The East Fork of Snow Creek is possibly the running water referred to. In the area on the north side of Hidden Lake that includes Long Valley, Round Valley, Tamarack Valley and San Jacinto Peak there is at present only one running stream, Snow and Falls Creeks. The East Fork Of Snow Creek begins on the headwall of Mount San Jacinto between that peak and Cornell Peak, to the east, and flows northward, joining the West Fork and West Branch of Snow Creek and Falls Creek, to the Coachella Valley and the mouth of the San Gorgonio Pass.

You ye va al (284)   Tahquitz Creek, Trail Crossing
"A steep, straight-down place--a place that makes one nervous"

This was "the next place down the ridge" on the way down from Lincoln Peak along the southwest ridge (Patencio 1943:97).

The place described is probably located just above the point where the old trail from Lincoln

Peak, down the southwest ridge of Lincoln Peak crosses Tahquitz Creek to join the trail that hugs the south wall of the canyon. The trail on the south wall can be followed from a point just above the first falls, but below the first falls the trail has apparently collapsed since earthquake, ca. 1948.

Yum ich you (286)   Thousand Palms Canyon & Village
"Brushy"

   Yum ich you is where the third and youngest son of *Ca wis ke on ca*, who was given the name, *Hes sou tem mem low it* (heart or bedrock), went to live with another tribe before moving on to yet another place (Patencio 1943:90).
   Some of the relations of the Palm Springs Indians who escaped from Seven Palms when it was attacked also went to Thousand Palms Canyon, which was probably the home of a lineage related to the *Kauisiktum* (Patencio 1943:89).

REFERENCES CITED

Anonymous
ca.   Cahuilla Sites in Northeastern San Diego County. Site records in files of L. J. Bean.
1938

Anthony, Frances
1901   At Indian Well. Land of Sunshine 13:235-240.

Baldwin, Clifford Park
1938   Toro Reservation Indian Wells. The Masterkey 12:151-153, 157.

Bancroft, Hubert Howe
1933   Guide to the Colorado Mines. California Historical Society Quarterly 12 (1):3-10. (Originally published 1863).

Barrows, David P.
1883-   The Coahuilla Indians. Manuscript, in file of L. J. Bean.
1900

1900   The Ethno-Botany of the Coahuilla Indians of Southern California. Chicago: University of Chicago Press.

Bean, Lowell John
1959   Field notes, in files of author.

1960   Cahuilla field notes, in files of author.

1960   The Wanakik Cahuilla. The Masterkey 34:111-120.

1966   California Fan Palm Sites. Manuscript, in files of author.

1972   Mukat's People: The Cahuilla Indians of Southern California. Berkeley: University of California Press.

1978   Cahuilla. In Handbook of North American Indians. Vol. 8 (California). William C. Sturtevant, gen, ed., Robert F. Heizer, vol. ed. Pp. 575-587. Washington: Smithsonian Institution.

Bean, Lowell John, and William Marvin Mason
1962   The Romero Expedition, 1823-1826. Los Angeles: Ward Ritchie Press.

Bean, Lowell John and Katherine Siva Saubel
1972   Temalpakh: Cahuilla Knowledge and Usage of Plants. Banning, California: Malki Museum Press.

Bean, Lowell John, and Sylvia Brakke Vane, eds.
1981   Native American places in the San Bernardino National Forest, San Bernardino and Riverside Counties, California. Report prepared for U.S. Forest Service South Zone Contracting Office, Arcadia, California, by Cultural Systems Research, Inc.

1983   Paniktum hemki: A Study of Cahuilla Cultural Resources in Andreas and Murray Canyons. Report prepared for Andreas Cove Country Club, by Cultural Systems Research, Inc.

1991   Unpublished Report on the Tahquitz Canyon Project. Report being prepared for the Riverside County Water and Flood Control District, by Cultural Systems Research.

Bean, Lowell John, and Sylvia Brakke Vane, and Jackson Young.
  1981   The Cahuilla and the Santa Rosa Mountain Region: Places and Their Native American Associations. Russell L. Kaldenberg, ed. Riverside California: Bureau of Land Management, California Desert District.

Beidler, Peter G.
  1977   Fig Tree John: An Indian in Fact and Fiction. Tucson: University of Arizona Press.

Benedict, Ruth
  1924   A Brief Sketch of Serrano Culture. American Anthropologist 26:366-392.

Blake, William P.
  1857   Geological Report. In Reports of Explorations in California for Railroad Routes to Connect with Routes Near the 35th and 32nd Parallels of North Latitude, Vol. V. Washington: Beverly Tucker, Printer.

Bright, William, and Jane Hill
  1967   The Linguistic Theory of the Cupeño. In Hymes, Dell H. (ed.). Studies in Southwestern Ethnolinguistics, pp 351-371. Mouton, The Hague.

Chase, J. Smeaton
  1919   California Desert Trails. Boston: Houghton Mifflin.

  1923   Araby: Palm Springs and Garden of the Sun. New York, New York: J.J. Little and Ives Company.

Curtis, Edward S.
  1926   The North American Indian, Vol. 15. Norwood, Massachusetts: Plimpton Press. (Johnson Reprint, New York, 1970.)

Drucker, Philip
  1937   Culture Element Distributions V: Southern California Anthropological Records 1:1-52.

Essig, E. O.
  1958   Insects and Mites of Western North America. New York: Macmillan.

Fairchild, Mahlon Dickerson
  1933   A trip to the Colorado mines in 1862. California Historical Society Quarterly 12:11-17.

Gifford, Edward Winslow
  1918   Clans and Moieties in Southern California. University of California Publications in American Archaeology and Ethnology 14:155-219.

Gunther, Jane Davies
  1984   Riverside County, California, Place Names: Their Origins and Their Stories. Rubidoux Printing Co.: Riverside, CA.

Hancock, Henry
  1880   Unpublished field notes of the United States Land Survey, San Bernardino Meridian. On file at the Riverside County Highway Department, Record Book 30:50. Riverside, California.

Henderson, Randall
  1941   Waterfall in Palm Canyon. Desert Magazine (January).

  1961   Let's Hike to Where the Palms Grow Wild: 10 Oases in the Canyons Above Palm Desert. Desert Magazine, April, 24-26.

Hill, Jane H., and Rosinad Nolasquez, ed.
  1973   Mulu'wetam: The First People. Banning, CA Malki Museum Press.

Hooper, Lucile
  1920   The Cahuilla Indians. University of California Publications in American Archaeology and Ethnology 16:315-380. (Reprinted in Studies in Cahuilla Culture, Malki Museum Press, Banning, California, 1978.)

Jaeger, Edmund C.
  1953   Forgotten Trails. Palm Springs Villager, September, pp. 12-14, 28.

James, George Wharton

1906   The Wonders of the Colorado Desert. Boston: Little, Brown and Company.

1908   Through Ramona's Country. Boston: Little, Brown.

1918   The Wonders of the Colorado Desert. Boston: Little, Brown.

Jefferys, Cheryl, Palm Springs Desert Museum

1990   Personal Communication, in CSRI files.

Johnson, John

1990   Personal Communication, in CSRI files.

Johnston, Francis J.

1960   Archaeological Problems of the Eastern Wanakik Territory. Manuscript in files of L. J. Bean.

1972   Stagecoach travel through the San Gorgonio Pass. Journal of the West, Vol. 11, No. 4.

1977   The Bradshaw Trail: Narrative and Notes. Riverside: Historical Commission Press.

Klein, Jack

n.d.   The Lady of the Palo Verde Tree. Los Angeles: Los Angeles Sunday Times.

Knack, M.

1981   Ethnography. In Cultural Resource Overview of the Colorado Desert Planning Units. Elizabeth von Till Warren, et. al. Pp. 83-105. Riverside: United States Bureau of Land Management Cultural Resources Publications, Anthropology/History (unnumbered).

Kroeber, A. L.

1907   Shoshonean Dialects of California. University of California Publications in American Archaeology and Ethnology 4:65-165.

1908   Ethnography of the Cahuilla Indians. University of California Publications in American Archaeology and Ethnology 4:65-165.

1925   Handbook of the Indians of California. Bureau of American Ethnology, Bulletin 78. (Dover Publications, New York, 1976).

La Croze, John

1856   Unpublished field notes of the United States Land Survey, San Bernardino Meridian. On file at the Riverside County Highway Department, Record Book 57:27. Riverside, California.

Lawton, Harry

1960   Willie Boy: A Desert Manhunt. Balboa Island, California: The Paisano Press.

Lawton, Harry, and Lowell John Bean

1968   A Preliminary Reconstruction of Aboriginal Agricultural Technology Among the Cahuilla. The Indian Historian 1(5):18-24, 29.

Lindsay, Lowell, and Diana Lindsay

1984   The Anza-Borrego Desert Region: A Guide to the State Park and Adjacent Areas. Berkeley, CA: Wilderness Press.

Meighan, Clement W.

1959   Varieties of Prehistoric Cultures in the Great Basin Region. Southwest Museum, Masterkey 33: 46-59.

Merriam, Clinton Hart

n.d.   Ethnographic Field Notes, on file at Bancroft Library, University of California, Berkeley.

Modesto, Ruby and Dave Modesto

1978   Personal communication, in CSRI files.

Patencio, Francisco
  1943   Stories and Legends of the Palm Springs Indians. Margaret Boynton, ed. Los Angeles: Times Mirror Company.

  1971   Desert Hours with Chief Patencio, as Told to Kate Collins by Chief Francisco Patencio. Roy F. Hudson, ed. Palm Springs Desert Museum.

Phillips, George Harwood
  1975   Chiefs and Challengers: Indian Resistance and Cooperation in Southern California. Berkeley: University of California Press.

Reed, Lester
  1963   Old Time Cattlemen and Other Pioneers of the Anza-Borrego Area. Benson, Arizona: Border-Mountain Press. (2nd edition, 1977)

Richter, Charles F
  1958   Elementary Seismology. San Francisco, CA: W.H. Freeman and Company.

Romero, John Bruno
  1954   The Botanical Lore of the California Indians. With Sidelights on Historical Incidents in California. New York: Vantage Press.

Ryan, R. M.
  1968   Mammals of Deep Canyon, Colorado Desert, California. Palm Springs, California: Palm Springs Desert museum.

Saunders, Charles Francis
  1913   Under the Sky in California. New York: McBride, Nast & Company.

  1914   With Flowers and Trees in California. New York: McBride, Nast & Company.

Schad, Jerry
  1986   A Foot and a Field: San Diego County. Berkeley, California: Wilderness Press.

Seiler, Hansjakob
  1970   Cahuilla Texts with an Introduction. Bloomington: Indiana University Language Science Monographs 6.

Shipek, Florence C.
  1977   A Strategy for Change: The Luiseño of Southern California. Ph.D. dissertation, University of Hawaii, Honolulu.

Smith, Desmond Mohler
  1942   The Effect of the Desiccation of Ancient Cahuilla Lake Upon the Culture and Distribution of Some of the Desert Indians of Southern California. M.A. thesis, University of Southern California, Los Angeles.

Smith, Wayland H.
  1909   In Re California Indians to Date. Los Angeles Council of the Sequoyah League Bulletin No. 5.

Steward, J. H.
  1929   Petroglyphs of California and Adjoining States. University of California Publications in American Archaeology and Ethnology 24:47-238.

Strong, William Duncun
  1929   Aboriginal Society in Southern California. University of California Publications in American Archaeology and Ethnology 26. (Malki Museum Press, Banning, California, 1972.)

Sutton, Mark Q.
  1988   Insects As Food: Aboriginal Entomophagy in the Great Basin. Ballena Press Anthropological Papers No. 33. Ed. Thomas C. Blackburn. Ballena Press: Menlo Park, CA.

Theilig, Eilene, Michael Womer, Ronald Papson
  1978   Geological Field Guide to the Salton Trough. In Aeolian Features of Southern California: A Comparative Planetary Geological Guidebook. Eds., Ronald Greenley, Michael Womer, Ronald Papson, Ann Spudis. Government Printing Office: Washington D.C.

U.S. Department of Interior, Bureau of Land Management
  1978   Ethnographic Notes 22.

U.S. Department of Commerce, Bureau of the Census
  1860

U.S. Department of War, U.S. Army Corps of Engineers
  1944

Vane, Sylvia Brakke
  1970   Field notes, in files of author.

  1979   Field notes, in CSRI files.

Walsh, Jane MacLaren
  1976   John Peabody Harrington: The Man and his California Indian Fieldnotes. Ramona, California: Ballena Press.

Wilke, Philip J.
  1976   Late Prehistoric Human Ecology at Lake Cahuilla, Coachella Valley, California. Ph.D. dissertation, University of California, Riverside.

Wright, William G.
  1884   A Naturalist in the Desert. Overland Monthly 4(21):279-284.

INDEX